Banana Bars & Ding-Dong Balls

For Lee and John —

True fans!

Banana Bats & Ding-Dong Balls

Go bananas!

Dan Gutman

A CENTURY OF
UNIQUE BASEBALL INVENTIONS

Dan Gutman

MACMILLAN • USA

MACMILLAN
A Prentice Hall Macmillan Company
15 Columbus Circle
New York, NY 10023

Library of Congress Cataloguing-in Publication Data
Gutman, Dan.
    Banana bats & ding-dong balls : a century of unique baseball inven-
tions / Dan Gutman.
      p.   cm.
    Includes bibliographical references (p.) and index.
    ISBN 0-02-014005-3
    1. Baseball—United States—Equipment and supplies—Anecdotes.
I. Title.   II. Title: Banana bats and ding-dong balls.
GV879.7.G88 1995
796.357'028—dc20   94-41609
                                           CIP

Manufactured in the United States of America
10 9 8 7 6 5 4 3 2 1

To Harold Berlin

In memory of Abner Doubleday, inventor of the fence post.

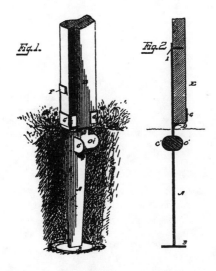

(No Model.)

A. D. DOUBLEDAY.

FENCE POST.

No. 310,800.   Patented Jan. 13, 1885.

Fig.1.

Fig.2.

It was irresistible fascination with an instrument of magic, a lure that belongs to all of baseball's paraphernalia. They are more than props for the daily drama: they bear the soul of the game itself.
—*Peter Richmond,* Baseball: The Perfect Game

Contents

Chapter 2   Practice   43

Ball-Thrower • The Baseball Gun • Why Do They Call Them "Iron Mike"? • The Modern Pitching Machine • The Perfect Swing • Swing Time • The Fingerprint of a Swing • The Artificial Curveball • The Bionic Pitcher • Ball Returners • How Fast? • The JUGS Gun • How Does It Work? • SuperVision • Danny Litwhiler: The Thomas Edison of Baseball • Litwhiler's Fly Swatter • The Instructional Bunting Bat • The Unbreakable Mirror • The Multiple Batting Cage • Diamond Dust • Diamond Grit • The Heavy Ball • The Lit-Picker • The Can't Release Golf Glove • Thomas Edison, Ballplayer • Ball Slinger • Bicycle Seat for Catchers • Slide-Rite • Heads Up! • Indoor Baseball

Chapter 3   Around the Ballpark   85

Bleachers • The Eighth Wonder of the World • The Plate • The Pitching Rubber • Field Marker • Where Are Our Inventors? • Ding-Dong Base • Electric Ding-Dong Base • Automatic Umpire • Why Do Umpires Use Whisk Brooms? • Indicators • Artificial Turf • Turf Facts • Tarpaulins • Fences • Turnstiles • The First Major League Night Game • The Megaphone Men • The First Electric Scoreboard • Telegraphic Baseball • The Vibrathrob • Telegraph Simulations • Radio Re-creations • Rhubarbs and Radios • Statistical Games • Computer Games • Rotisserie • Mechanical Baseball Bank • The Personal Computer • The Baseball Computer • The Future of Baseball Simulation • Buy Me Some Peanuts and . . . • They Always Taste Better at the Ballpark • Beer and Coke • For the Fan Who Has Everything

Acknowledgments

Some people never return your calls. Others drop everything to help an author in need. The following people opened their hearts and file cabinets to assist in collecting the information and images found in these pages:

James Anderson of the Photographic Archives at the University of Louisville; Nat Andriani of the Associated Press; Aarne Anton of American Primitive Gallery; Andrew Attaway; Allen Barra; at the Baseball Hall of Fame, Bill Deane, Pat Kelly, Patrick Donnelly, Leigh Connor, Bob Browning, Dan Cunningham, and Gary Van Allen; Steve Baum; Philip E. Von Borries; John S. Bowman; George Brace; Jeanine Bucek; James A. Calhoun of Wilson Sporting Goods; Jack Carlson; Joan Curtis of the Cherry Hill Public Library; Michelle D'amaco; Steve Davis; Dave Dempsey at Electronic Arts; Dick Derby of Yannigan's; Ray Dimetrosky; Morris Eckhouse and John Zajc of the Society for American Baseball Research; Rick Elstein; Josh Evans at Leland's; Bob and Ann Feller; Mindy Savar Fendrick of Franklin Electronic Publishers; Arthur Goldstein of Collector's Stadium; Earle Halstead; Jess Heald of Worth, Inc.; J. Thomas Hetrick; Susy Hoffman and Jean Washko at Borden; Bill Jaspersohn; Gerald Jesselli; Jack Kavanagh; David Kelly of The Library of Congress; Bob Kuenster of *Baseball Digest;* Mike Lattman;

Elizabeth Law; Len Levin; Robert Edward Lifson of Robert Edward Auctions; Danny Litwhiler; Elizabeth Lowther and Zandra Moberg at the Patent Collection of the Free Library of Philadelphia; Mike McGraw and Ed Milner of Balsam; Rob McMahon; Dave Mullany of The Wiffle Ball, Inc.; at the New York Public Library, Charlotte Dixon, Dominick Pilla, and Wayne Furman; Butch Paulson, Rob Nelson, and Gary McGraw at JUGS; David Plaut; Howard M. Pollack; Doug Rauschenberger of the Haddonfield Public Library; Mitch Rose; Alan "Mr. Mint" Rosen; Ed Rouh; Dyanne DeSalvo Ryan; Patty Shaw; Scott Smith and Ruth Zayas of Rawlings; Robert W. Smith of Harry M. Stevens, Inc.; Mike Sparrow of the Cleveland Public Library; Mark Steffens of S.T.A.R.T. Technologies; Chuck Stevens; Pam Stone and Shirley Brisbois of Spalding; Douglas Tarr of the Edison National Historic Site; Paula Throp at ATEC; Tom Tresh; Frank Vizard of *Popular Mechanics*; Chris Welch; Rich Wescott; Bill Williams of Hillerich & Bradsby; Nanci Young of The Seeley G. Mudd Manuscript Library at Princeton University.

Special thanks go to three people: My wife, Nina, for her support (and free illustrations); my agent, Brian Zevnik, who went above and beyond the call of duty; my editor, Rick Wolff, who raised an eyebrow with interest when I desperately tossed out this wacky book idea after he had shot down five ideas *I* thought were good.

Introduction

About a millisecond after the first pitch was thrown, some guy un-
doubtedly muttered under his breath, "*I* can make a better baseball than *that.*"

An instant later, when the first bat was swung, somebody surely
thought, "*I* can carve a better bat than *that.*"

And after that first fly ball was gathered in by some anonymous outfielder, a third fan certainly proclaimed, "Why, that fella could catch a *lot*
better if he was wearing a glove—and *I'm* just the guy to make one!"

Americans love gadgets. We're fascinated by anything new and better, and we suffer from a national inability to ever be satisfied. Civiliza-
tion's earliest tools—a stick and a rock—provided all that was necessary
for a game of baseball (that was *truly* the dead ball era). But the game
was developed and improved at the same time as America was jumping
headfirst into the Second Industrial Revolution—1875–1900.

It was a time of incredible spirit of invention. The nation had reached
its one-hundredth birthday. Independent inventors were changing the
way people would live, and Yankee ingenuity was applied to The National Pastime just as it was to agriculture, communications, transporta-
tion, and warfare. Virtually all of baseball's tools would be created
within this short period of time. By 1893 we had figured out how to
mass produce just about anything.

While Alexander Graham Bell was in Boston diddling with the first telephone in 1876, Frederick Winthrop Thayer was just across the river in Cambridge, bending wire for the first catcher's mask. While Orville and Wilbur Wright were perfecting their glider in 1897, Professor Charles "Bull" Hinton was perfecting his mechanical pitching machine. While Henry Ford was building his automobile empire, Albert Spalding (seen here) was building his sporting goods monopoly.

Figure 1-1A   *(National Baseball Library, Cooperstown, New York)*

Inventors rarely receive credit, but they played an enormous role in making baseball what it is. The "lively ball era" didn't come about just because somebody said, "Hey, let's make the game lively." It came about because Ben Shibe invented machines that could wind yarn tightly and uniformly around a cork-centered ball. The invention of the mask and mitt enabled catchers to move up behind the plate and become the field generals of the game. The inventions of telegraphy, radio, and television brought the game to a mass audience. The invention of artificial turf made the game faster and changed it in ways that we both cheer and deplore.

Somehow, I can't imagine that football fans care who invented the inflatable bladder. I doubt hockey fans have an interest in the history of the puck. But I suspect that baseball fans, obsessives as we are, want to know about the geniuses who dreamed up shin guards, JUGS guns, jockstraps, flip-up sunglasses, aluminum bats, the Wiffle Ball, and baseball's other weird and wonderful paraphernalia.

And because baseball is a game in which even superstars fail seven times out of ten, baseball inventions that *didn't* make it are worthy of our attention—bats shaped like question marks, bases with bells in them, inflatable batting helmets and radio-controlled catcher's mitts. Maybe the inventors of these failures were simply ahead of their time. After all, the parachute was invented 300 years before the airplane.

I hope I haven't written a (yawn) *History of Sporting Goods in America*. The idea here, as with most baseball books, is to tell a bunch of cool stories you probably haven't heard before.

—*Dan Gutman, 1995*

Invention

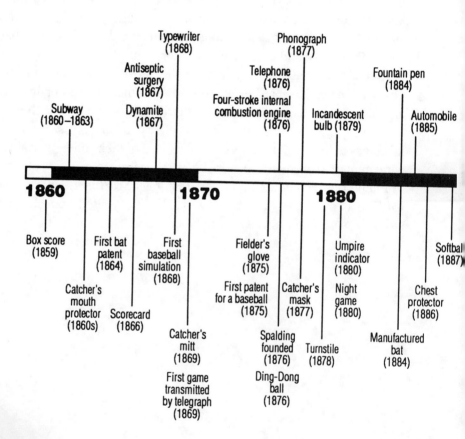

Subway
(1860–1863)

Antiseptic
surgery
(1867)

Dynamite
(1867)

Typewriter
(1868)

Four-stroke internal
combustion engine
(1876)

Telephone
(1876)

Phonograph
(1877)

Incandescent
bulb (1879)

Fountain pen
(1884)

Automobile
(1885)

1860　　　　　　　**1870**　　　　　　**1880**

Box score
(1859)

First bat
patent
(1864)

First
baseball
simulation
(1868)

Fielder's
glove
(1875)

Umpire
indicator
(1880)

Softball
(1887)

Catcher's
mouth
protector
(1860s)

Scorecard
(1866)

First patent
for a baseball
(1875)

Catcher's
mask
(1877)

Night
game
(1880)

Chest
protector
(1886)

Catcher's
mitt
(1869)

Spalding
founded
(1876)

Turnstile
(1878)

Manufactured
bat
(1884)

First game
transmitted
by telegraph
(1869)

Ding-Dong
ball
(1876)

and Baseball

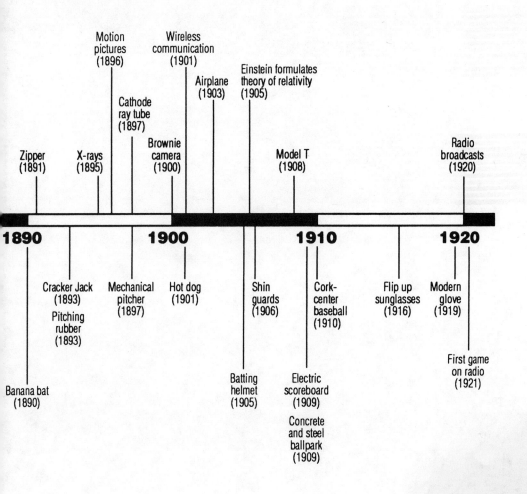

Motion pictures (1896)

Wireless communication (1901)

Einstein formulates theory of relativity (1905)

Airplane (1903)

Cathode ray tube (1897)

Brownie camera (1900)

Radio broadcasts (1920)

Zipper (1891)

X-rays (1895)

Model T (1908)

1890

1900

1910

1920

Cracker Jack (1893)

Mechanical pitcher (1897)

Hot dog (1901)

Shin guards (1906)

Cork-center baseball (1910)

Flip up sunglasses (1916)

Modern glove (1919)

Pitching rubber (1893)

Banana bat (1890)

Batting helmet (1905)

Electric scoreboard (1909)

First game on radio (1921)

Concrete and steel ballpark (1909)

Bats

The first baseball bat was certainly a tree branch, stripped of its bark and whittled lovingly by some caveman slugger until it felt just right in his hands.

That's the way it was done for a long time. Bats were homemade, carved out of many different kinds of wood and in all shapes. Gradually, players learned that a round bat made of white ash hit a ball the hardest.

Legend has it that when the Ohio State Penitentiary was being dismantled in 1880, a player named Perring took a plank of hickory from the gallows scaffold and hand-carved it into a baseball bat. It gave him a feeling of power to step to the plate with a piece of wood that had been used to hang men.

Joe, Dom, and Vince DiMaggio, the story goes, made baseball bats out of oars from their father's fishing boat.

Probably the last homemade bat was "Wonderboy," the fictional club Roy Hobbs wielded in *The Natural*. He carved it from a tree hit by lightning and carried it around in a bassoon case. When the bat finally broke, Hobbs buried it in the outfield. In the movie version, they used a Louisville Slugger.

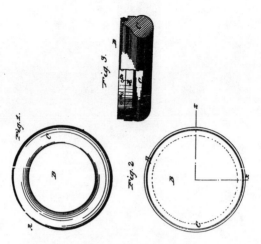

P. CAMINONI.
BAT FOR CRICKET, &c.
No. 42,834. Patented May 24, 1864.

Figure 1-1 *(U.S. Patent Office)*

▲ **The Ass Bat, 1864.** *Figure 1-1* This is the first United States patent issued for a bat. Alexander Cartwright had written the first formal rules to baseball 19 years earlier, and many people still hadn't heard of the new game. In his patent application, inventor Philip Caminoni of New York City said his bat was for "cricket and other similar plays."

Caminoni certainly had a unique idea. His bat was made from a wood frame covered by "the skin of an ass, swine, or other animal." That's what I'd call killing animals for sport! Hundreds of baseball bat patents would follow this one, some of them even more bizarre.

▶ **Pete Browning, the Original Louisville Slugger.** *Figure 1-2* The birth of the manufactured baseball bat took place in Louisville, Kentucky, in 1884. During a game one day, Pete "The Gladiator" Browning broke his favorite bat. Browning was a star outfielder of the Louisville Eclipses in the American Association, and a career .343 hitter.

After the game, a teenage boy named John Andrew "Bud" Hillerich invited Browning home, promising to make the slugger a new bat. Hillerich's father was a woodworker who manufactured bedposts, butter churns, and porch railings.

Figure 1-2 *(Hillerich & Bradsby Company)*

With Browning watching from behind, Bud Hillerich took a piece of white ash and shaped it into a baseball bat on his father's lathe. Every few minutes, he removed the bat from the lathe and Browning took a practice swing or two.

"Take a mite off here and a mite off there," he instructed Hillerich, until the bat felt perfect. The next day Pete used it in a game and went three for three.

"There's no future in supplying an article for a mere game," J. Fred Hillerich told his son. But Pete Browning's teammates started asking Hillerich to make *them* bats, and soon players from other teams passing through Louisville did the same. Hillerich & Son was in the baseball bat business.

More than a century later, Hillerich & Bradsby is still the largest wooden bat manufacturer in the world. There isn't much call for butter churns anymore.

▼ **The World's First Bat Factory.**   *Figure 1-3*   In this 1887 photo, J. Fred Hillerich is the man with the long beard on the left. Bud Hillerich is in the doorway, on the right. The other men were Hillerich employees. Note the butter churn on the ground and the bedpost in the doorway.

▼ *Figure 1-4*   J. F. Hillerich & Son considered calling their bat "Falls City Slugger" but settled on "Louisville Slugger" instead. The name was trademarked in 1894—Pete Browning's last season.

In 1911, a salesman named Frank Bradsby joined J. F. Hillerich &

Figure 1-4   *(University of Louisville Photographic Archives)*

Figure 1-3
(University of Louisville Photographic Archives)

Son. He was so successful that in 1916 the firm's name was changed to Hillerich & Bradsby.

Bud Hillerich, who turned the first Louisville Slugger as a boy, died in 1946. The Hillerich family still runs the company today.

▲ **Baseball's First Flake.**   Pete Browning had a number of idiosyncrasies. A student of hitting, he would "retire" a bat after he had made a specific number of hits with it. Consequently, he had hundreds of bats lying around, and he gave each of them a name. He also believed he could make his batting eye stronger by staring into the sun for extended periods of time.

A heavy drinker, Pete was known for the wise saying, "I can't hit the ball until I hit the bottle." (If only they'd had beer commercials in those days!)

Browning *looked* funny. His eyebrows were so thick, friends suggested that he might hit better if he trimmed them.

It should come as no surprise that Pete eventually went crazy and was committed to an insane asylum near Louisville. He was released in 1905 and died the same year. He was 44. Oddly enough, two of Pete's teammates—Chicken Wolf and Philip Reccius—spent time in the same insane asylum.

Eccentricity ran in the Browning family—Pete's nephew Tod Browning was the director of the 1932 cult film classic *Freaks,* which starred circus sideshow performers demonstrating their physical abnormalities.

▲ **Two Pete Browning Stories.**   Hall of Fame manager John McGraw played third base in his playing days. When there was a runner on third in a tag-up situation, McGraw was known to grab the guy's belt from the back to make him fall on his face.

One day Pete Browning reached third with one out. He had fallen for McGraw's trick before. This time Pete loosened his belt. When the batter hit a fly ball, Browning tagged up and scampered home holding his pants up, while McGraw was left standing at third with Browning's belt in his hand.

But don't give Pete *too* much credit for smarts. Another oft-quoted Browning story is of the time somebody informed him that James Garfield had been assassinated. Browning's response: "Oh, yeah? What league was he in?"

▼ *Figures 1-5A, B, C*   A baseball bat cost about a dollar before the turn of the century. It was often sold with a guarantee card—if the bat broke, it could be returned.

Figures 1-5A,B,C

Figures 1-6A,B

▲ **Early Recycling.** *Figures 1-6A, B* Spalding ran these ads in 1887–1888. In the days before the assembly line and mass production, it was not unusual for a manufacturer to solicit the public for wood to make into baseball bats. As America switched from the horse and buggy to the automobile, "tongues" from old wagon wheels were the perfect resource to be recycled into baseball bats.

▲ **Bat Rules.** Until 1852, there were no restrictions on baseball bats. A guy could lug a piano leg to the plate if he wanted to. In 1859, it was ruled that bats could be any length, but no larger than 2.5 inches in diameter. Ten years later, the length was limited to 42 inches, and in 1895 the diameter increased to 2.75 inches. That's the way it has remained for the last century.

▼ **Going Batty (Men and Their Bats).** *Figure 1-7* Hall of Famer Cap Anson, pictured here, owned about 500 bats. He hung them in his cellar like cheeses. When he spotted an interesting-looking fencepost or log, he would buy it and have it made into a bat.

Frank Frisch hung his bats in a barn during the off-season. Eddie

Figure 1-7   *(National Baseball Library, Cooperstown, New York)*

Collins buried his in a dunghill. Honus Wagner boiled his bats in creosote. Jimmy Frey soaked his in motor oil. Joe DiMaggio rubbed his bats with olive oil. Germany Schaefer would *bite* a new bat to test the wood. Joe Jackson took his bat, which he named "Black Betsy," to bed with him. Al Bumbry named one of his bats "My Soul Pole."

▲ **You Can Never Be Too Thin.** Early baseball bats were almost as fat at the handle as they were at the barrel. It must have been like swinging a log. Bats began to slim down around the turn of the century. Rogers Hornsby is usually cited as the first player to use a truly tapered bat.

According to Hillerich & Bradsby, 36-ounce bats were the norm before 1950. In those days, it was believed that the heavier the bat, the farther a hitter could drive a ball.

In today's "lite" era, we know it's the exact opposite. Physicists have proven that bat *speed* plays a larger role in how far the ball travels than bat *weight.* The faster you can swing the bat, the farther you hit the ball. And the lighter the bat, the faster you swing. Major leaguers swing their bats 110–120 mph.

It has also been argued that pitchers have become stronger and fastballs faster, so hitters have switched to lighter bats out of necessity. It's simply too hard to get a heavy bat around on 90-mph-plus heat.

Bats dropped to 34–35 ounces in the 1950s. Today, bats that weigh 31–32 ounces are in the greatest demand. Five-time batting champ Tony Gwynn used a featherweight 31-inch, 30-ounce bat.

Great hitters like Ted Williams, Rod Carew, and Stan Musial used light bats, in the range of 31–33 ounces. Roger Maris whacked his 61 home runs in 1961 with a 33-ounce bat. Hank Aaron was known for using one of the lightest bats in the game, and he hit more home runs than anybody. In his final year even Babe Ruth—who once swung a 42-ounce club—was swinging 35 ounces.

WACKY BATS

▶ **The Paper Bat, 1884.** *Figure 1-8* Yes, *paper,* compressed and shaped in a mold. "My object is to furnish a base-ball bat which will not be liable to break or split in the hands of the player," wrote inventor

William Williams of Huntington, Pennsylvania, "and which at the same time will possess the requisite qualities of density, elasticity, and withal economy of construction." Another example of early recycling. Williams's bat also foreshadowed baseball's future, because he suggested his bat could be reinforced by molding the paper around a metallic core.

▶ **The Flat Bat, 1889.** *Figure 1-9* Bats with one flattened side were legalized in 1885. Usually, players planed off one side of a round bat, but Charles Morris of Cincinnati patented this bat that became progressively more oval up the barrel.

"The bat here described possesses the advantage of more effective and accurate hitting and of discretionary presentation of the 'flat' of the bat, either squarely or obliquely, according to the kind of 'ball' and the idiosyncrasies of the pitcher."

Flat bats were banned in 1893, but a century later they're coming back. An Irvine, California, company called Bio-Kinetics is experimenting with an oval bat. They claim it can be gripped better because it doesn't turn in the hitter's hand.

▶ **The Exploding Bat, 1902.** *Figure 1-10* Ninety years have failed to reveal what John Schwanengel could have possibly been thinking when he invented this bat. The Dayton, Ohio, man suggested boring a hole in the barrel of the bat and a smaller hole inside the first hole. An exploding cartridge was inserted in the small hole, a metallic hammer in the larger one. When the bat hit a ball over the holes, an explosion would result.

"The object of my invention," wrote Schwanengel, "is to produce an explosive effect to amuse juveniles." Perhaps Vince Coleman would have used it.

It's only a matter of time before somebody does the same thing with a computer chip that produces baseball sound effects.

▶ **The Banana Bat, 1890–1906.** *Figures 1-11A, B* Probably baseball's strangest invention. Emile Kinst was a man with a mission—to spread the gospel of the curved baseball bat, which he believed would improve the game.

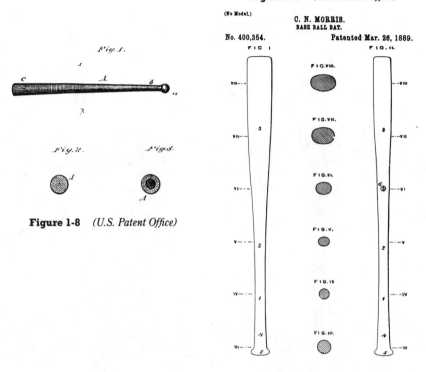

(No Model.)

W. WILLIAMS.
BASE BALL BAT.
No. 292,190.   Patented Jan. 22, 1884.

Fig. 1.

Fig. 2.   Fig. 3.

Figure 1-8   *(U.S. Patent Office)*

Figure 1-9   *(U.S. Patent Office)*

(No Model.)

C. N. MORRIS.
BASE BALL BAT.
No. 400,354.   Patented Mar. 26, 1889.

No. 708,261.   Patented Sept. 2, 1902.

J. C. SCHWANENGEL.
BALL BAT AND EXPLOSIVE.
(Application filed Mar. 24, 1902.)

(No Model.)

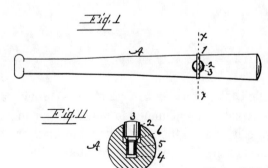

Fig. 1

Fig. 11

Figure 1-10   *(U.S. Patent Office)*

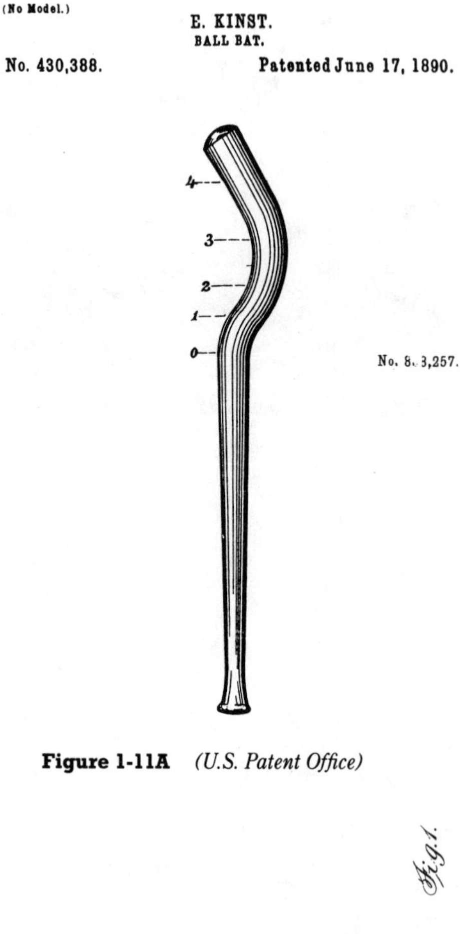

Figure 1-11A   *(U.S. Patent Office)*

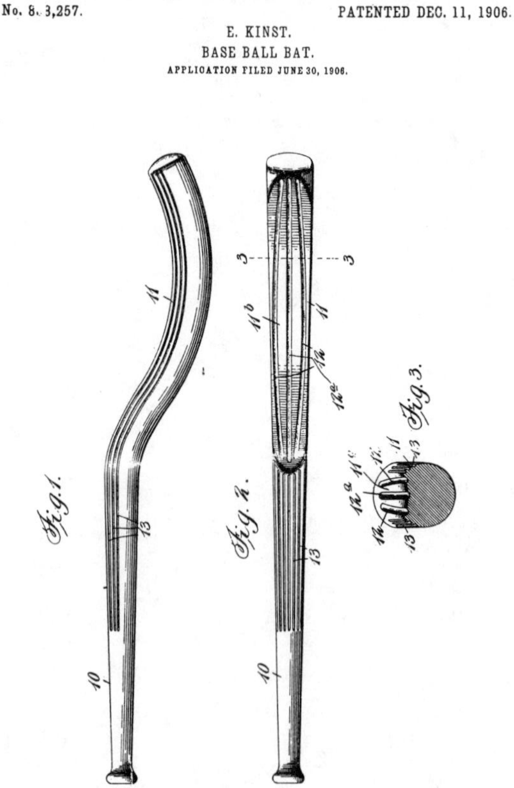

Figure 1-11B   *(U.S. Patent Office)*

"The object of my invention," the Chicago man wrote, "is to provide a ball-bat which shall produce a rotary or spinning motion of the ball in its flight … and thus to make it more difficult to catch the ball, or, if caught, to hold it." Kinst also insisted that his bat would enable hitters to drive the ball more easily to all parts of the field.

"Owing to the peculiar form of my bat, the game becomes more difficult to play, and therefore much more interesting and exciting, because
the innings will not be so easily attained, and consequently the time of
the game will also be shortened."

The Major League Rules Committee, needless to say, nixed the banana bat.

▼ **The Big Bend Bat.** *Figure 1-12A* Maybe Kinst wasn't so crazy
after all. In 1977, an East Peoria man named John Bennett was sweeping
a floor when the thought crossed his mind that a *bent* broom might give
him more efficiency. Bennett constructed a broom with a 19-degree
bend in the middle and indeed found it was easier to use than a straight
broom. He quickly tried the same thing with a hammer, fishing rod, skil-
let, wheelbarrow, and baseball bat.

The idea was that holding the bat with its "elbow" pointing toward the

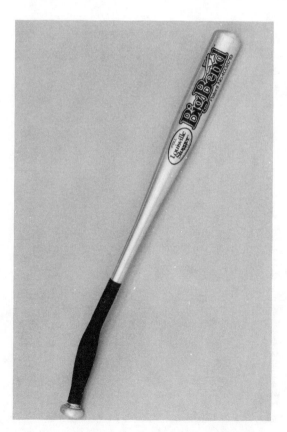

Figure 1-12A *(Hillerich & Bradsby Company)*

pitcher would prevent early or late "rollover" of the wrists. Furthermore, a hitter could get it around faster than a straight bat.

Bennett's bat played in Peoria, and it was advertised as "the most revolutionary breakthrough since the invention of the wheel." He sold the idea to Hillerich & Bradsby in 1981, who marketed it under the name "Big Bend."

"You'd expect to see a drunk bat with this thing," wrote Tom Barnidge in the *St. Louis Post Dispatch.*

▼ **The Bedpost Bat.** *Figure 1-12B* This is the creation of Jess Heald, the chairman of Worth, one of today's largest bat manufacturers. Heald's idea was that the hills and valleys down the length of the bat would create a more random line of flight, which would make it harder for fielders to predict where the ball would go.

Figure 1-12B *(Hillerich & Bradsby Company)*

The bat was never put on the market. "I still have it sitting in my closet," Heald says.

If you think the bedpost bat is odd, you should see another of Heald's offbeat baseball brainstorms—a collapsible bat. The handle slid into the barrel, sort of like a telescope. It cut the length of the bat in half. "You could fold it up and put it in your pocket," according to Heald.

Jess Heald has had some *good* ideas too, such as the aluminum bat (end of this chapter) and the RIF ball (see Chapter 4).

▲ **The Knobby Bat.**   Around the turn of the century Wright & Ditson manufactured a bat with *two* knobs—one at the end and another about six inches up the handle. Many hitters of the day, including Ty Cobb and Honus Wagner, hit with their hands apart. So with this bat they could hold one hand on each knob. The bat was endorsed by Napoleon Lajoie (.422 in 1901) and sold as "The Double Ring Handle."

▶ **The Bottle Bat.**   *Figure 1-13A*   Cincinnati Reds third baseman Heinie Groh became famous for using this bat, which he said gave him better control. You can't argue with him (he died in 1968, for one thing) because he averaged .292 over 16 seasons. After hitting .474 in the 1922 World Series, Heinie got a "474" license plate for his car.

"The topography and geography of this bat," explained *Baseball Magazine* in 1920, "is strikingly similar to that of the containers formerly used for the encasement of John Barleycorn and his kind."

The bottle bat had a brief resurgence in the 1970s. George Foster of the Cincinnati Reds (next page) experimented with one, but never used it in a game. One of Groh's original bottle bats was used as a prop in Woody Allen's movie *Zelig*, and it was accidentally broken during filming.

▲ **Weighted Bats.**   Even in the days when hitters preferred heavy bats, they wanted them to *feel* light. Typically, they would take practice swings with an armful of bats and when they discarded all but one, it felt like a toothpick. It didn't take long for weighted bats to come along.

In the 1930s, some players drilled holes in their bats and filled them with lead. The weighted "donut" came into use in the 1960s and was popularized by Elston Howard. For a while Hillerich & Bradsby sold a bat called "Whip-O-Warm-Up." The barrel was made of rubber.

▼ **The Amazing Bat-O-Matic.** *Figure 1-14* The manufacturer called this "the most effective and ingenius invention of all time for athletes." Basically, it was a plastic bat with a transparent barrel that had a shaft down the middle. Hitters, using the thin shaft as their visual guide, would supposedly learn to *aim* their swings more accurately.

The manufacturer, prone to hyperbole, also claimed Bat-O-Matic would give hitters a *mental* edge. "Psychologically it will put tension on the opposing pitcher," reads the brochure. "Pitchers, facing clubs known to be using Bat-O-Matic, will be aware that the club using it has a definite advantage. More power at the plate and publicity will put psychological pressure on the pitchers facing such a club." *Right.*

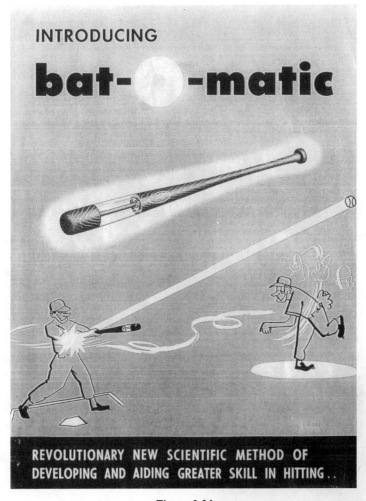

Figure 1-14

▼ **How Long Does a Bat Last?**   *Figure 1-15*   Babe Ruth hit 21 of his 60 homers in 1927 with the same bat. We know this because Ruth used to carve a notch around the trademark of his bat every time he slugged a home run with it.

A baseball bat can last a long time. Hall of Famer Joe Sewell used just one in his entire 14-year career, stroking 2,226 hits with it.

It's unlikely that any modern player could keep a bat so long. Thinner handles and inferior wood make bats snap like twigs. Jim Rice, it is said, once swung a bat so hard that it broke in half—even though he missed the ball *entirely*. Major leaguers today go through as many as six dozen bats in a season.

Figure 1-15   *(National Baseball Library, Cooperstown, NY)*

Figure 1-16A
(George Brace)

Figure 1-16B
(George Brace)

Figure 1-16C
(George Brace)

Figure 1-16D
(George Brace)

▲ **Size Counts.** *Figures 1-16A, B, C, D* In the history of major league baseball, the player with the distinction of wielding the *longest* bat was Hall of Famer Al "Bucketfoot" Simmons (top left), who lugged a 38-inch weapon to the plate. The shortest was Wee Willie Keeler's (top right) 30.5-inch bat (of course, Wee Willie wasn't much bigger than that *himself*). Their lifetime batting averages were similar—.334 and .343, respectively. But Simmons hit 307 homers to Keeler's 34.

The heaviest bat—48 ounces—belonged to Edd Roush (bottom left), the Hall of Fame outfielder with the New York Giants and Cincinnati Reds. Solly Hemus (bottom right) used the lightest bat ever—29 ounces. He hit .304 with it in 1954.

Figure 1-17   *(George Brace)*

▲ **The Zebra Bat.**   *Figure 1-17*   St. Louis Browns left fielder Leon "Goose" Goslin arrived for the 1932 season with his "war club"—a bat with 12 green stripes around it. On Opening Day he walked up to the plate with the thing and the umpires declared it to be distracting and illegal.

Goslin managed to hit .299 for the year with a normal bat. He was inducted into the Hall of Fame in 1968.

▼ **The Semi-Automatic Fungo Bat.** *Figure 1-18* The art of fungo-ing is difficult to master. Inventors never tire of dreaming up ways to flip the ball in the air without having to remove one hand from the bat. Phillip Knott of New York City patented this bat, within which a series of balls were loaded and ready for hitting. You'd just jam the bellows be-tween your hands and fluid pressure would cause a ball to pop out the barrel. After six fungoes, it was time to reload.

Nobody knows for sure, incidentally, where the term "fungo" came from. It's been in use since at least 1886. *The Dickson Baseball Dictio-nary* provides five theories, the most unusual one being that "fungo" is derived from "fungus." Practice bats, so they say, used to be so soft that they seemed to be made of fungus. Next theory . . .

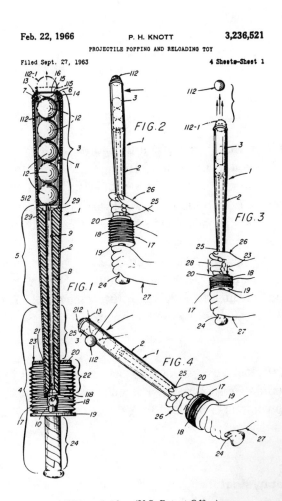

Figure 1-18 *(U.S. Patent Office)*

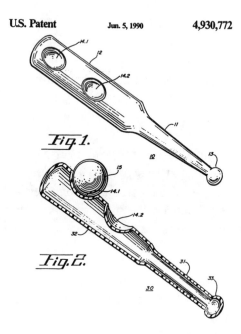

U.S. Patent   Jun. 5, 1990   4,930,772

Fig.1.

Fig.2.

Figure 1-19   *(U.S. Patent Office)*

▲ **No, This Was Not Pete Gray's Fungo Bat.**   *Figure 1-19*   Inventors Michael Maloney and Linda Watson of Bloomington, Minnesota, had another solution to the fungo problem. They carved baseball-shaped scoops into the top of the bat barrel. The hitter would simply raise the bat to loft the ball a few feet in the air, move the bat into hitting position, and swing away.

Notice the bat has *two* scoops. The outer scoop was intended for hitting deep fly balls, the inner one for grounders. Or, you could put a ball in *each* scoop and hit two fungoes at the same time. That innovation could put a lot of coaches on unemployment.

▶ *Figure 1-20*   Instead of scooping wood out of the bat to hold a ball, Canadian Conrad Genjack devised a small cup that he strapped to the bat. The cup could also be used for catching a ball, as you can see in "Figure 2."

▲ **The Metaphysical Bat.**   In 1977, a Brooklyn man named Joe Martino invented an extra-thick bat with a *hole* cut through it right where

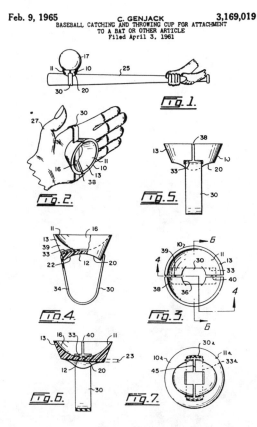

Feb. 9, 1965   C. GENJACK   3,169,019
BASEBALL CATCHING AND THROWING CUP FOR ATTACHMENT
TO A BAT OR OTHER ARTICLE
Filed April 3, 1961

Figure 1-20   *(U.S. Patent Office)*

the "sweet spot" would be. So if a batter hit a ball perfectly, *he wouldn't hit it at all*—it would go right through the bat!

A home run would be a strikeout! The worse you hit the ball, the *better* you would hit the ball! Baseball, unfortunately, is no place for existentialism and Martino's bat never caught on.

ILLEGAL BATS

▶ *Figure 1-21* Fixing bats before they break is a time-honored baseball tradition. Ted Kluszewski (right, with the arms) used to bang tenpenny nails into his bat barrels to make them harder and heavier. George Sisler filled his bats with Victrola needles.

Figure 1-21 *(National Baseball Library, Cooperstown, NY)*

When players learned that a *lighter* bat could hit a ball farther than a heavy bat, they started drilling holes in the barrels of their bats and filling them with cork, foam, or some other lighter-than-wood material.

▶ **The First Corked Bat.** *Figure 1-22* Actually, the loaded bat is *not* a new idea. Charles F. Held of St. Louis patented this one back in 1903. Held wasn't thinking long ball.

"The object of this invention is to construct a base-ball bat with two longitudinal holes arranged near its periphery to provide means for bunting the ball when desired and also for lightening said bat," he wrote. By facing the holes toward the pitcher, Held believed, the batter

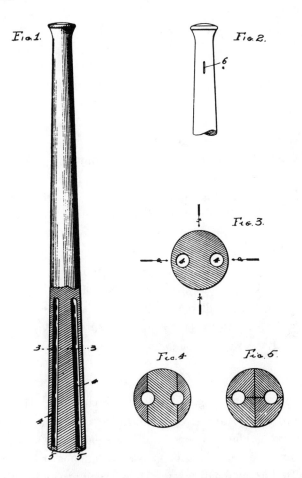

No. 727,359.

PATENTED MAY 5, 1903.

C. F. HELD.
BASE BALL BAT.
APPLICATION FILED SEPT. 8, 1902.

NO MODEL.

Fig.1.

Fig.2.

Fig.3.

Fig.4.

Fig.5.

Figure 1-22 *(U.S. Patent Office)*

"is enabled to drop the ball closer to him than he could should he strike it on the solid side."

Held didn't ignore the fact that the rules of baseball require that hitters use a solid piece of wood. As his patent indicates, "Plugs 5 are then placed in the holes, concealing them from view."

▲ **Confirmed Corkers.** After their careers were over, Amos Otis and Norm Cash admitted using corked bats. Cash hit .361 in 1961, winning the American League batting title.

California Angel Dan Ford was ejected from a game in 1981 when umpires discovered his bat was corked. Billy Hatcher of the Houston Astros was suspended for ten days in 1987. Graig Nettles took a swing once and six Super Balls rained across the infield of Yankee Stadium. An interesting way to cheat.

Nettles told of a teammate in the minors who inserted a tube of *mercury* into his bat. When the bat was held upright, it felt very light. But when he swung it, the centrifugal force caused the mercury to rush up the barrel, moving the center of gravity and making the bat swing like a bludgeon.

Unfortunately, Captain Mercury couldn't get his miracle bat on the ball. He never made it to the majors.

In 1982, *Sport Magazine* reported an anonymous Chicago hitter inserted three metal rods down one side of his bat. When he swung the bat rods-down, it would increase the chances of hitting a fly ball. With the bat rods-up, a grounder could be purposely hit. Too bad the bat couldn't do the one thing hitters *want* to do when they step to the plate—hit a line drive.

The most accused bat corker in recent memory is Howard Johnson of the New York Mets. Johnson, who had hit 12-11-10 home runs in 1984–1986, suddenly walloped 36-24-36 in 1987–1989. Opposing managers started checking his bats regularly. But like those taken of Dizzy Dean's head, the X-rays revealed nothing.

▶ **The Cupped Bat.** *Figure 1-23* In the late 1930s, Hanna Manufacturing Company of Athens, Georgia, manufactured a bat in which an ounce of wood had been scooped out of the end in the shape of a teacup. The company went out of business in 1976, just a year after cupped bats were legalized in the major leagues. Lou Brock was one of the first players to use one. Johnny Bench is pictured with one here.

Cupped bats have a slightly altered center of gravity, but it has not been proven that they drive a ball harder or farther than conventional bats.

BIRTH OF A BAT

Baseball bats grow on trees, white ash trees. Hillerich & Bradsby owns 5,000 acres of them in Pennsylvania and upstate New York. Years ago, "old hickory" was used, but ash is lighter, more resilient, and one

Figure 1-23   *(National Baseball Library, Cooperstown, NY)*

of the strongest woods for its weight. It also replenishes itself quickly
enough so there's no need to plant new trees.

The best wood for a baseball bat comes from trees on a north- or east-
facing slope of a hill. The soil is richer there, so trees grow closer together and are forced to grow straight and tall.

Figure 1-24 *(Hillerich & Bradsby Company)*

▲ *Figure 1-24* When a tree reaches approximately 60 years of age or 12 inches in diameter, it is chopped down and cut into "billets"—40-inch cylinders. H&B cuts about 40,000 trees a year, the average tree yielding 60 billets. These are shipped to the Hillerich & Bradsby factory in Indiana, across the Ohio River from Louisville.

▶ *Figure 1-25* The billets are dried for four to six weeks in H&B's hot-air kilns. If wood is dried too quickly, the fibers rupture, weakening the bat. After the drying process, the billets are graded. For every 10 billets, only one is good enough to be made into a professional bat. These usually come from the "butt piece" of the tree, which is lowest on the trunk.

The grain of the wood also determines the quality of the bat. Very tightly packed grain makes a weak bat because the wood fibers don't bind together well. Very wide grain makes a brittle bat.

Next, the billets are sorted by weight and ready for carving. Two billets that are exactly the same size may be up to 10 ounces apart in weight.

Figure 1-25   *(Hillerich & Bradsby Company)*

▶ *Figure 1-26* Nowadays, less than 5 percent of all bats are turned by hand—only particularly unusual models. An automatic lathe used for batmaking has 28 knives on it, and each one has to be adjusted individually to carve any of 213 bat shapes. It takes a couple of hours to set all the knives, but once they're in place the lathe can turn out a bat in just 15 seconds.

The five most popular bat models are always set up and ready to go on automatic "tracer lathes," which use a metal template of the bat

Figure 1-26   *(Hillerich & Bradsby Company)*

shape. They work much like the machine locksmiths use to cut duplicate keys.

Hillerich & Bradsby keeps records of the bat specifications for every major leaguer, down to the millimeter. This information is carefully guarded. Roughly 70 percent of today's major leaguers use H&B bats.

▶ *Figures 1-27A, B*   After the bat is perfectly shaped, it's branded with the distinctive oval Louisville Slugger trademark and a player's autograph. Then it's sanded lightly.

A bat's model number is usually keyed to the player's name. Babe Ruth, for instance, used a Louisville Slugger Model R43. Lou Gehrig used Model GE 69.

▶ *Figure 1-28*   Finally, the bat is dipped in finish. Hillerich & Bradsby has half a dozen finishes. "The Walker finish" was named for Harry Walker, who, looking for new bats at the Louisville factory, found that

Figure 1-27A *(University of Louisville Photographic Archives)*

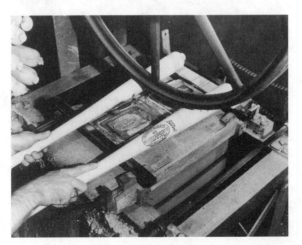

Figure 1-27B *(Hillerich & Bradsby Company)*

the only one to his liking was being used to stir a vat of brown varnish. A very dark finish was preferred by George Foster, and came to be called "The Foster finish."

Some players, such as Robin Ventura and Darryl Strawberry, like to

Figure 1-28   *(Hillerich & Bradsby Company)*

hit with raw wood. In these cases, the bat is rotated briefly over an open gas flame to bring out the grain.

A guy that makes $5 million a year doesn't have to pay for his own bat. His team does—$22.50 for each one.

▶ **Sluggers Can Be Choosers.**   *Figure 1-29*   Over the years, many players have made pilgrimages to the Hillerich & Bradsby factory to personally pick through the lumber and select bats for the coming season. Babe Ruth liked wood with knots in it. Ted Williams (pictured here) searched for narrow-grained wood. He would drop a billet on a concrete floor and listen to the sound to determine if the bat was right for him.

Williams was known for making fine distinctions between bats. He could pick the one bat out of six that was half an ounce heavier. Once, he returned a set of bats with a note saying, "Grip doesn't feel just right." The bats were measured and found to be .005 of an inch thinner than Williams had ordered.

Figure 1-29 *(University of Louisville Photographic Archives)*

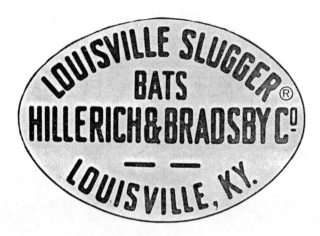

Figure 1-30   *(Hillerich & Bradsby Company)*

▲ **Trademark Up!**   *Figure 1-30*   Players once carved their initials in their bats to distinguish them from those of their teammates. In 1905, Honus Wagner signed a contract with Hillerich & Bradsby to become the first player to have his signature burned into the wood of his bats.

Batters from Little League on up have always been instructed to hold a wooden bat with the trademark facing *up.* It's not just superstition. Bat-makers brand the trademark on the side of the bat nearest the sapwood of the tree, or the "flat of the grain." So when the trademark is facing the sky, the strongest part of the wood will hit the ball.

Even major leaguers ignore this age-old advice. Yogi Berra was so adamant about holding his bats with the trademark facing the pitcher that Hillerich & Bradsby began stamping Yogi's bats with the trademark on the *wrong* side *intentionally.*

Career home run champ Hank Aaron had the last word on the trademark issue. When an opposing catcher helpfully suggested that Aaron hold his bat with the trademark facing up, Hammerin' Hank responded curtly, "I didn't come up here to read."

▶ **The Bat Mobile.**   *Figure 1-31*   Every spring, this double trailer goes around to major league training camps. Inside are machinery and Rawlings technicians trained to hand-turn bats and repair gloves while-u-wait.

Figure 1-31 *(Rawlings Sporting Goods)*

THE NONWOOD BAT

In the mid-1800s, an Oberlin College student named Charles Martin Hall attended a lecture in which his chemistry teacher told the class that anyone who invented a commercial process for making aluminum would make a bundle. Hall leaned over to the student next to him and whispered, "I'll be that man."

In 1886, Charles Martin Hall patented the aluminum process. It was just two years after Bud Hillerich turned the first Louisville Slugger.*

Hillerich & Bradsby used to make seven million wooden baseball bats a year. This year they'll make a little over *one* million, plus the same number of aluminum bats. Nonwood bats are taking over baseball, and most experts believe that even the major leagues will be using them soon.

*Aluminum is made from bauxite, which makes up 8 percent of the Earth's crust and is one of the planet's most abundant metals. Your aluminum bat probably originated in Jamaica, a major exporter of bauxite.

"I certainly see a time in the not-too-distant future when everyone will be using some alternative bat—aluminum, graphite, or some composite," says Jack Hillerich, president of Hillerich & Bradsby.

Nobody did much with Charles Martin Hall's creation until World War II, when the aerospace industry began searching for a strong, light substance that could be used to build faster planes.

During the late 1960s, a Pennsylvania manufacturer of aluminum pool cues named Anthony Merola got the idea of fashioning a thicker tube and seeing if it might work as a baseball bat. It did. He set up a small manufacturing operation, and the bat was approved by several softball associations in 1969.

Merola didn't stick with the bat-making business, but Worth, Inc., a Tennessee baseball manufacturer that had been founded in 1912, heard about his aluminum bat. They had been thinking of expanding into baseball bats and saw nonwood as the wave of the future.

Instead of bringing in a bat-making expert, Worth hired Jess Heald, an aerospace engineer who knew a thing or two about metal alloys. In 1970, Worth introduced its first aluminum bat, a beet-red softball bat with a black end plug. They sold 10,000 of them for $9.95 each. Easton Sports, in Burlingame, California, was right behind. The two companies have been the market leaders ever since. Jess Heald is now Worth's chairman of the board.

Aluminum was approved for Little League play in 1971, and the NCAA gave it the okay for college baseball in 1974. By 1975, aluminum bat sales had surpassed wood. Today, aluminum makes up more than 75 percent of the bat market.

The biggest reason baseball is making the switch is simple—wood breaks, aluminum doesn't.* According to Worth, their bats will withstand 10,000 impacts against a thrown baseball. Wood bats rarely survive more than 250 impacts, and sometimes they crack on the *first* one (hold that trademark *up!*).

For budget-conscious schools and Little Leagues, it made sense to switch from wood to metal. It has also been argued that aluminum

---

*Actually, it *does*. After a certain amount of wear, aluminum suffers metal fatigue stress, which causes small cracks. The stress is "stored" in the metal, and it's a cumulative effect. In other words, the bat doesn't "heal" if you put it in the closet over the off-season. Aluminum bats have been known to break in half after years of use.

is *safer* than wood, which can splinter and seriously injure a player.

The other reason the wooden bat is going the way of the dinosaur is that nonwood bats *perform* better. This is obvious to anyone who has tried hitting with a wood bat and then picked up an aluminum bat. The ball *jumps* off the bat like a bullet. You feel like Babe Ruth.

An aluminum bat is lighter, so the hitter swings it faster and hits the ball harder. And because the bat is hollow, its center of gravity is closer to the hands. This makes a larger sweet spot and a more forgiving bat. When you miss the sweet spot of a wood bat, the ball dribbles away. With an aluminum bat you can miss the sweet spot and still hit the ball over the fence.

"We can make a bat that's three to five ounces lighter with a sweet spot three times larger than any wood bat," says Jess Heald. "We can even put that sweet spot right where we want it."

Baseball purists who complain that aluminum is replacing wood are behind the times—because now *graphite* is replacing *aluminum*. The first graphite homer was hit by Dwight Evans of the Red Sox during batting practice on March 12, 1987.

Graphite is a plentiful carbon mineral, which until now was known mainly as the "lead" in pencils. It's even stronger and lighter than aluminum. A graphite bat can survive the impact of 300 baseballs shot from an air cannon at 180 mph. Aluminum breaks down at 75–150 impacts, and wood can't stand up to a single pitch at that speed.

According to *Popular Science* magazine, graphite bats are made of "triaxially braided graphite fibers that are layed up by hand over a mandrel, or rod, and consolidated in a mold injected with thermoset epoxy resin."

Wasn't it so much easier when they just chain-sawed trees?

Today, batmakers are engaged in an arms race, leapfrogging each other as lighter aerospace alloys and high-tensile-strength tubing materials are developed. Worth is currently experimenting with titanium-alloy bats, which are said to hit harder than graphite.

▶ *Figure 1-32* Aside from respect for tradition, there is real fear in baseball circles that nonwood bats are dangerous (because they hit so hard), are unfair (because they make weak hitters look better than they are), and change the physics of the game and the nature of the pitcher/batter confrontation so much that 100 years of baseball statistics will become meaningless.

U.S. Patent May 19, 1992 Sheet 1 of 2 5,114,144

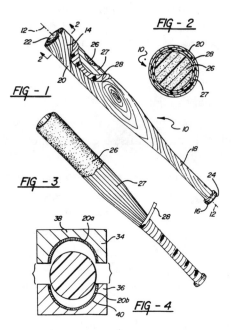

Figure 1-32 *(U.S. Patent Office)*

"If aluminum gets to the majors," says Wade Boggs, "I'm certain there will be another .400 hitter."

Batmakers are addressing that problem. It is now possible, they say, to build a synthetic, unbreakable bat that perfectly duplicates the performance of wood, right down to the *craaaaaak* upon impact.

In fact, a Michigan man named Steven Baum has invented a synthetic bat that even *looks* like wood. His "BaumBat" (seen here) is made of a plastic-foam core surrounded by two crisscrossing layers of resin-impregnated synthetic fibers, all of which is covered by an ash "veneer." The only way you can tell a BaumBat isn't solid wood is by noticing it hasn't cracked after 3,000 hits. BaumBat has been tested by 14 major league teams. The Burlington Indians used them exclusively during the 1993 season, and they won the Appalachian League pennant.

▲ Worth's PowerCell bat and Titan Blue Dot ball are "tuned" to one another. The impact compression and rebound of the two are matched for an enhanced energy return effect that produces "the maximum hit distance."

▼ **The Birth of an Aluminum Bat.** *Figure 1-33* At the Worth factory in Tullahoma, Tennessee, they start with a round, seamless tube of "aircraft aluminum." The metal is just 70-thousandths to 75-thousandths of an inch thick. Machines push it under high pressure through a die, which works something like squeezing toothpaste out of a tube.

▼ *Figure 1-34* The material is then formed into the shape of a bat using a "swedging" process in which the taper and handle sections are formed into one "unibody" design. The first aluminum bats were made of several pieces, but in 1973 Jess Heald patented a one-piece model that was safer and easier to make.

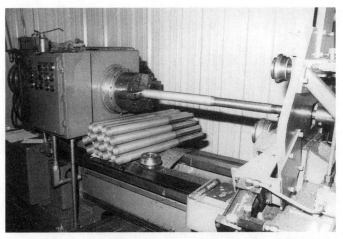

Figure 1-33 *(Worth)*

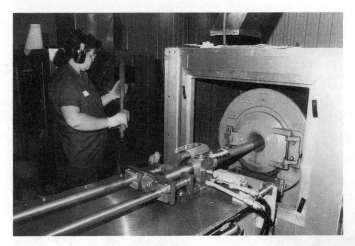

Figure 1-34 *(Worth)*

Figure 1-35   (Worth)

▲ *Figure 1-35*   Next, the bat is subjected to the heat of a 900-degree oven and quickly plunged into a cold-water bath that drops it down to room temperature in seconds. This greatly increases the strength of the metal.

▼ *Figure 1-36*   Foam plastic material is then stuffed inside for sound-deadening purposes, and the knob is welded to the body. Finally, the bat gets a light sanding and buffing, and the finish and lettering are applied.

Figure 1-36   (Worth)

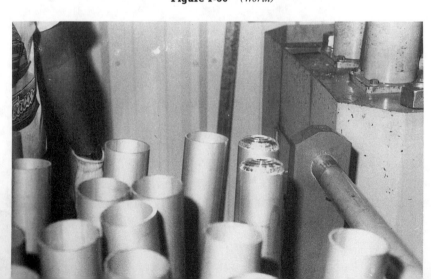

▲ Incredibly, nonwood bats have become *traditional*. When Worth introduced its graphite bat, it had the option of making the bat sound like the *crack* of wood or the *ping* of aluminum. Worth chose the latter.

"The kids playing today never used wood," explains Jess Heald. "Wood sounds dead to them."

So the sound of aluminum striking a baseball, which is so annoying to older fans, is the sound of *power* to the next generation of baseball players and watchers.

"By the turn of the century even the majors will probably have put down the lumber and picked up the metal," writes *Sports Illustrated*. "Like it or not, the *crack* of the bat is inevitably being replaced by a *ping*."

2

Practice

First, I shall demonstrate the difficulty of hitting against my machine. . . . The public will see that men cannot best science, but science can perfect men.
—Princeton professor Linton before a demonstration of his pitching machine, in Luke Salisbury's novel *The Cleveland Indian.*

HITTING PRACTICE

1894 . . . 1994. A hundred years haven't made a tremendous difference in personal batting-practice devices. There's only so much you can do with a string, a ball, and a frame to dangle the ball at waist level.

Solo batting-practice devices are useful, but can never duplicate the action of swinging at a pitched ball. Because skilled pitchers are not always available, over the last 100 years many inventors developed machines that could hurl a baseball mechanically. There have been *hun-*

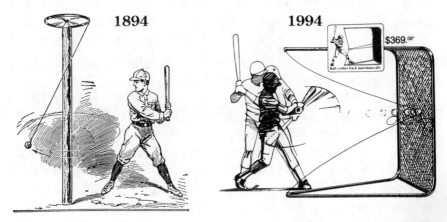

1894   1994 $369.⁰⁰*

Figure 2-1A *(Spalding's Official Base Ball Guide)*   **Figure 2-1B**   *(Sport-Star Company)*

dreds of pitching machines, employing everything from springs and rubber bands to compressed air, catapults, centrifugal force, and explosives.

▶ **Ball-Thrower, 1876.** *Figure 2-2* One of the first attempts at a throwing machine was this slingshot patented by Ira A. Paine of New York City the same year the National League was founded. But Paine's device, basically an elastic cord and cup, was intended to be used for practicing pigeon shooting.

▶ **The Baseball Gun.** *Figures 2-3A, B, C* The first "practical" pitching machine was the "Dummy Pitcher," invented by Professor Charles Howard "Bull" Hinton (the obvious inspiration for the Professor Linton quoted at the start of this chapter).

An odd sort, Hinton fled England in 1887 after being charged with bigamy. He spent a few years in Japan, then came to America where he somehow landed a position teaching mathematics at Princeton University. There, Hinton became known for his theory of a four-dimensional universe. The professor used clever stories such as this to illustrate mathematics: "Suppose you have four boys and one pie. If you want to divide the pie equally each boy will have one-quarter of the pie. If there are two boys, each will have one half of the pie. If one boy, he will have the whole pie. But if there is only half a boy, he will have two pies, which is manifestly impossible, as there is only one pie."

Anyway, Hinton was also a baseball fan and decided to do something about the pathetic Princeton team. He theorized that the hitters were having trouble because they rarely had the opportunity to practice against good pitchers. Hinton resolved not only to build a pitching machine, but to build a machine that could throw *curveballs*.

His first idea was to pattern the machine after a catapult, but he quickly abandoned that idea. "No catapult has yet been built," Hinton said, "which can impart a rotary motion to the projectile, thus causing a curve." He was right. Instead, Hinton based his machine on a gun.

While other Princeton professors were teaching classes and grading papers, Hinton constructed a large-bore toy cannon that would shoot baseballs. With each pitch, a loud explosion of gunpowder set off a cylinder of compressed air, which propelled the ball in the general direction of home plate. The terrified hitter was required to step on an elec-

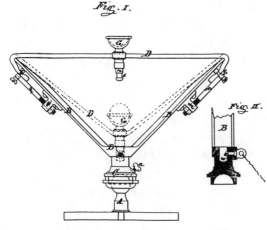

I. A. PAINE.
BALL-THROWER.

No. 175,870.   Patented April 11, 1876.

Fig. I.

Fig. II.

Figure 2-2   *(U.S. Patent Office)*

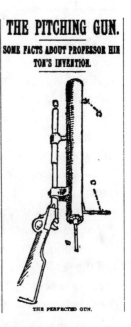

THE PITCHING GUN.

SOME FACTS ABOUT PROFESSOR HIN TON'S INVENTION.

THE PERFECTED GUN.

Figures 2-3A,B,C   *(The Cincinnati Enquirer)*

"DUMMY" PITCHER TRIED.

SPECIAL DISPATCH TO THE ENQUIRER.

MEMPHIS, TENN., August 13.—The mechanical pitching gun which a Princeton University professor patented recently was given a trial here to-day in the game between the Chickasaws and Nashvilles. The gun pitched two innings for each club, and no runs resulted, the game ending 4 to 3 for the local team. The gun struck out the first two men up, and but one ball was hit outside the diamond. Over a thousand people witnessed the "dummy" pitcher throw out curves, speed and drops with perfection control.

GETTING ONTO THE "DUMMY."

SPECIAL DISPATCH TO THE ENQUIRER.

MEMPHIS, TENN., August 14.—The mechanical baseball gun or dummy pitcher was given a second trial here to-day in the game between the Chickasaws and Nashvilles. The players found its curves easier to connect with than during the first day, but in two innings the dummy struck out two men and allowed three hits. Prof. Hinton, the inventor, has an idea that his machine will take the place of pitchers in the preliminary spring batting practice, and from local results the gun should prove a success for practicing batters.

tric switch to set the thing off—somewhat like orchestrating his own execution by firing squad. Unfortunately, no photos of the machine survive.

To throw a fastball, Hinton placed the ball at the rear of the barrel so it received the full force of the explosion. For a change-up, the ball was placed closer to the front of the barrel.

The tough pitch for the machine, as for humans, was the curveball. First, Hinton tried roughing up one side of the barrel to put a spin on the ball. Then he tried winding the ball with ribbon, which would unwind as the ball left the gun. Neither idea worked.

Finally, Hinton hit on the idea of using three rubber-coated iron "fingers" inside the gun barrel. When the baseball shot past the fingers, they impeded the motion on one side, causing the necessary spin.

Hinton's first test in the Princeton gym on December 15, 1896, was somewhat of a sensation. Over the next few years he put on demonstrations for many people (including Mrs. Grover Cleveland), culminating in a highly publicized game on August 13, 1900, in Memphis. The machine put in a good performance, as can be seen in these clips from *The Cincinnati Enquirer.* The only problem was that the gun took so much time to reload that it never went longer than three innings. It might have made a good short reliever, though.

To the students of Princeton, Bull Hinton was most famous for the time somebody tried to snatch a yellow chrysanthemum from his coat and the professor threw the man over a fence. Hinton never patented his pitching machine (though the first clip says he did), which was strange considering that after leaving Princeton he became an examiner in the patent office in Washington. Hinton died on April 30, 1904.

▶ *Figure 2-4* Pitching machines patterned after cannons were noisy, slow, and dangerous, but the idea persisted. In 1902 a Navy ship carpenter named Robert Howard Lake applied for a patent on his "mechanical ball thrower." It took six years for it to be approved.

Lake used no explosive charge, relying exclusively on a tank of compressed air (P) to propel the ball at the batter. Instead of iron fingers, he used a flexible strap around the ball (r) to throw curves. Or, as Lake put it, "to impart thereto a twisting movement about an axis transverse to its line of flight."

The machine, it was claimed, could make a ball curve eight feet. That's highly unlikely. In more recent years Dr. Lyman J. Briggs of the

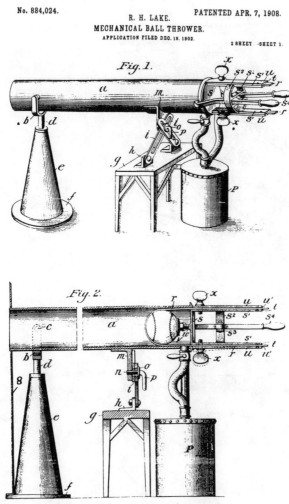

No. 884,024.

R. H. LAKE.
MECHANICAL BALL THROWER.
APPLICATION FILED DEC. 18. 1902.

PATENTED APR. 7, 1908.

2 SHEET -SHEET 1.

Figure 2-4   *(U.S. Patent Office)*

National Bureau of Standards calculated that the maximum distance a baseball can curve is 17.5 inches.

But Lake's machine did address one criticism all pitching machines receive—they don't help the hitter follow a pitcher's *delivery*. The machine was designed to work alongside a human pitcher, and would shoot the ball while the pitcher pantomimed a throwing motion.

▶ *Figure 2-5A*   There would be other baseball throwing cannons, but pitching machine inventors gradually reverted to the technology the cannon had made obsolete—the catapult, which was developed by the

M. E. KOEHLER.
APPARATUS FOR MECHANICALLY THROWING A BASE BALL.
APPLICATION FILED MAR. 1, 1915.

1,152,186. Patented Aug. 31, 1915.
3 SHEETS—SHEET 1.

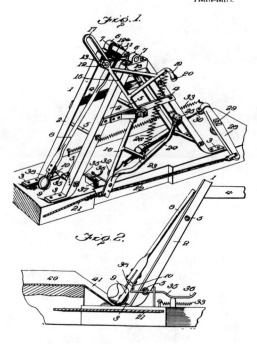

Figure 2-5A *(U.S. Patent Office)* 1,211,738.

B. N. MARTY.
AUTOMATIC BASE BALL PITCHING MACHINE.
APPLICATION FILED APR. 29, 1916.

Patented Jan. 9, 1917.
2 SHEETS—SHEET 1.

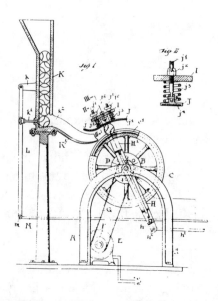

Figure 2-5B *(U.S. Patent Office)*

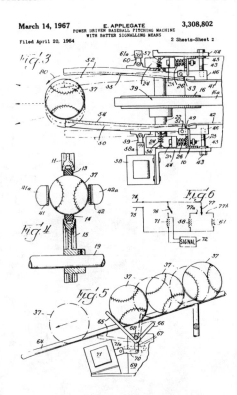

March 14, 1967   E. APPLEGATE   3,308,802
POWER DRIVEN BASEBALL PITCHING MACHINE
WITH BATTER SIGNALLING MEANS

Filed April 20, 1964   2 Sheets—Sheet 2

Figure 2-5C   *(U.S. Patent Office)*

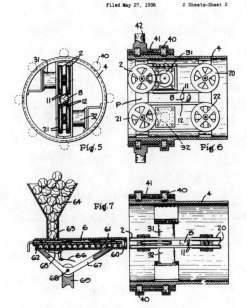

March 29, 1938.   H. I. SNIPPEN   2,112,611
BALL THROWING DEVICE

Filed May 27, 1936   2 Sheets—Sheet 2

Figure 2-5D   *(U.S. Patent Office)*

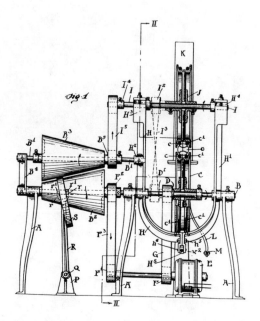

B. N. MARTY.
AUTOMATIC BASE BALL PITCHING MACHINE.
APPLICATION FILED APR. 29, 1916.

1,204,468.

Patented Nov. 14, 1916.
2 SHEETS—SHEET 1.

Figure 2-5E   *(U.S. Patent Office)*

Greeks around 350 B.C. to heave rocks. This 1915 model, invented by Maxemillian Koehler of Spokane, was typical of early catapult pitching machines.

In the coming years, catapult machines would become increasingly sophisticated, as you can see from these patents (figures 2-5B, C, D, E). Some used motor-driven pulleys to build up tension on a spring, which whipped the arm around and released the ball with a slight backspin.

Catapults can't throw curveballs, however.

▶ *Figure 2-6* Cleveland manager Lou Boudreau and coach George Susce tinkering with a pitching machine during spring training in 1942. This one was modeled after a crossbow.

▶ *Figure 2-7* The first major league team to use a pitching machine regularly was the Brooklyn Dodgers during the late 1940s. In this 1950 photo, Dodger pitcher Rex Barney faces his mechanical counterpart.

Figure 2-6 *(National Baseball Library, Cooperstown, NY)*

Figure 2-7 *(AP/Wide World Photos)*

▲ **Why Do They Call Them "Iron Mike"?**   The 1950 Wake Forest College baseball team named their pitching machine "Iron Mike," probably in honor of Joe "Iron Man" McGinnity. The Hall of Fame pitcher was famous for tirelessly working (and frequently winning) both games of doubleheaders.

The nickname spread after newspapers covered a game between Wake Forest and North Carolina State in which Iron Mike did all the pitching for both teams. For the sake of the machine, balks and stolen bases were prohibited. Wake Forest won 8–0, slamming three homers off Mike.

▼ **The Modern Pitching Machine.**   *Figure 2-8*   In 1950, a Detroit policeman named Eliot B. Wilson stumbled upon a discovery that would revolutionize the mechanical pitching machine. Wilson found that when he placed a ball between two automobile tires spinning rapidly in opposite directions, the ball *shot* out the other side as if it had been thrown very hard. He received this patent for his "ball throwing device" in 1956, but didn't do much with it.

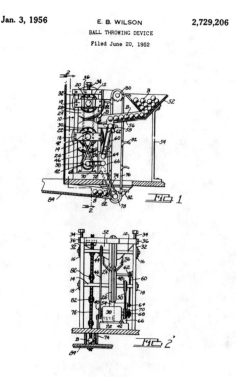

Jan. 3, 1956   E. B. WILSON   2,729,206
BALL THROWING DEVICE
Filed June 20, 1952

Figure 2-8   *(U.S. Patent Office)*

▼ *Figure 2-9A* Fifteen years after Wilson's discovery, an Oregon man named John Paulson had a problem—his 12-year-old son Butch couldn't hit a curveball. Paulson (seen here) looked at the pitching machines that were available in the early 1970s and decided he could build a better one. He purchased Wilson's patent and improved on it to create the JUGS Curveball Pitching Machine.

The machine was named after the "jug handle curve," and Paulson also named his company JUGS, Inc. He got a patent of his own, which is reproduced here (figure 2-9B).

The beauty of using spinning wheels to throw a ball is that they make it possible to manipulate the spin on the ball so any pitch imaginable can be thrown. If both wheels turn at the same rate, the ball shoots out with

Figure 2-9A   *(JUGS, Inc.)*

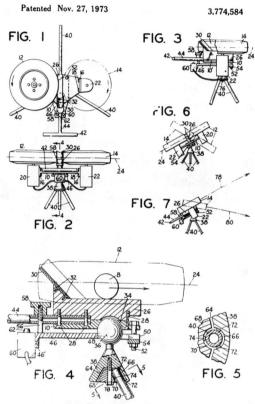

Patented Nov. 27, 1973   3,774,584

Figure 2-9B   *(U.S. Patent Office)*

no spin—a knuckleball. If the wheels turn at different rates and the machine is tilted on various planes, a fastball, curve, slider, or screwball can be thrown. Today, nearly all mechanical pitchers employ spinning wheels.

Point the machine *away* from the plate and it can throw grounders, pop-ups, and fly balls for fielding practice—600 of them an hour. Pitching machines have fired baseballs at 150 mph and bounced them off the roof of the Astrodome. They've even been used to fire ice balls at aluminum siding to simulate hail.

Recently, pitching machines have become the hip gift for the wealthy. Barbara Mandrell bought one. Jane Fonda bought one for her kids. For his birthday in 1993, David Letterman received one.

The same technology used to throw a baseball is also used to practice soccer, field hockey, lacrosse, tennis, and cricket. JUGS, Inc., makes a football passing machine that can throw a perfect spiral over 100 yards.

John Paulson died in March 1984. Today the president of JUGS, Inc., is Butch Paulson—the kid who couldn't hit a curveball.

▼ *Figures 2-10A, B, C, D* JUGS's biggest competitor is ATEC (Athletic Training Equipment Company), which was also founded in Oregon in the 1970s. Its most popular pitching machines are "Casey" (left), which is used by the pros, and "Rookie" (right), a favorite of amateur leagues.

Most of ATEC's equipment was invented by Larry Ponza (see 2-10D), a former engineer for Lockheed and McDonnell-Douglas who patented his first pitching machine in 1952. Ponza is now retired but still works for ATEC as a consultant.

Figure 2-10A *(ATEC)*

U.S. Patent   Apr. 15, 1980   4,197,827

Figure 2-10B   *(U.S. Patent Office)*

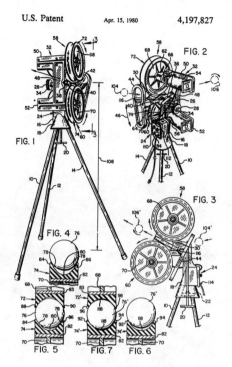

U.S. Patent   Apr. 1, 1980   Sheet 2 of 4   4,195,614

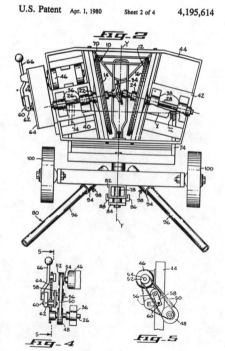

Figure 2-10C   *(U.S. Patent Office)*

Figure 2-10D *(ATEC)*

▲ Mechanical pitchers never get a sore arm, you never have to send them to the showers or renegotiate their contracts at midseason, and they never get caught with drugs. But their biggest advantage is not the practice they give major league hitters—it's the practice they give the *next* generation of hitters.

Instead of getting ten swings a day against some out-of-shape coach who can't get the ball over, for the first time kids can regularly practice the difficult art of hitting a baseball. ATEC owns Grand Slam U.S.A., a chain of more than 80 batting ranges across the country. Every weekend boys *and* girls swarm to these cages to hit against pitching machines for hours.

JUGS sponsors youth leagues in which machines do all the pitching. This way, kids don't blow out their arms, pitches are always over the plate, and games are faster, safer, and more action-packed. The down side of mechanical pitchers is that every year or so a kid will walk in front of one. Fatalities have resulted.

Figure 2-11A1   *(ATEC)*

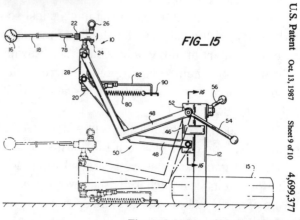

FIG_15

U.S. Patent   Oct. 13, 1987   Sheet 9 of 10   4,699,377

Figure 2-11A2   *(U.S. Patent Office)*

▼ *Figures 2-11A1, 2-11A2; 2-11B1, 2-11B2* Two of Larry Ponza's other inventions. "Swing King" (left) is a fixed ball on a movable tee that teaches bat control. "Soft Toss" (below) helps develop eye/hand coordination. It also doubles as an automatic ball feeder for a pitching machine.

Figure 2-11B1 *(ATEC)*

U.S. Patent   Jun. 30, 1987   Sheet 1 of 3   4,676,504

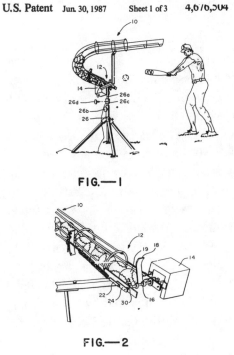

FIG.—1

FIG.—2

Figure 2-11B2 *(U.S. Patent Office)*

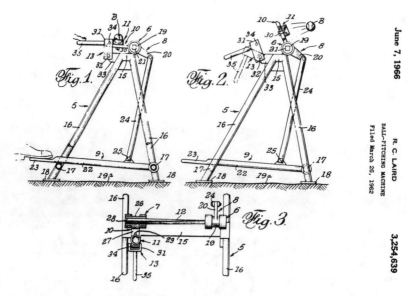

June 7, 1966

R. C. LAIRD
BALL-PITCHING MACHINE
Filed March 26, 1962

3,254,639

Figure 2-12   *(U.S. Patent Office)*

▲ *Figure 2-12*   Who needs explosives, compressed air, or rotating tires when you can just step on a pedal? This human-powered mechanical pitcher, invented by Roy Laird of Palmdale, California, was marketed under the name "Chucker."

▶ **The Perfect Swing.**   *Figures 2-13A, B*   Now that the mechanical pitching machine has essentially been perfected, inventors have turned their attention to the swing itself. The emergence of the computer has made a number of high-tech devices possible to help hitters analyze their swings, detect flaws, and correct them.

The stick figures shown here are actually New York Yankee star Don Mattingly. They were created by a computerized motion-analysis system from Bio-Kinetics of Irvine, California. First, the hitter (or pitcher) is photographed with two video cameras in which the shutters open and close in a thousandth of a second. From that video, a computer generates animated three-dimensional stick figures like the ones here.

Bio-Kinetics, which was founded by ex-pitcher Tom House, has built a visual database of more than 100 professional ballplayers for comparison purposes. A similar system is sold by Peak Performance Technologies, a company founded by biomechanics specialists at the U.S. Olympic Training Center in Colorado.

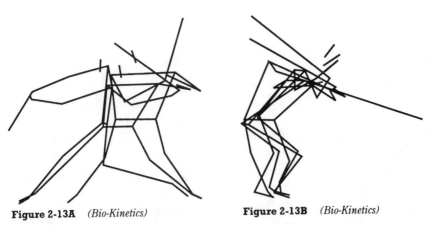

Figure 2-13A   *(Bio-Kinetics)*   **Figure 2-13B**   *(Bio-Kinetics)*

▼ **Swing Time.**   *Figure 2-14*   The distance a batted ball travels is determined by body mass and bat speed. It wouldn't be practical to gain 50 pounds to become a power hitter, but a simple adjustment in a hitter's swing can add 10 mph to his bat speed—which means an extra 40 feet to the distance of a fly ball.

Quick Bat, made by Sport-Star of Portland, Oregon, measures bat speed. A reflective sticker on the end of the bat trips two optical sensors during the swing. Quick Bat calculates the speed in miles per hour and flashes it instantly. This way a hitter can change his stance, stride, or grip and see how it affects the speed of his swing. Versions of the device sell for $149 to $340.

Figure 2-14   *(Sport-Star Company)*

According to Sport-Star, the highest recorded bat speed is 116 mph, though Sport-Star did not record the name of the player who achieved that mark. Most hitters are in the 60- to 75-mph range. The graph shows how fast a hitter should swing, depending on body weight.

▼ **The Fingerprint of a Swing.**   *Figures 2-15A, B*   The first swing is a "batprint" of a poor swing, the second is a pro swing. Both were created using the Batronic Bat Swing Analyzer from Sportronix of Hatboro, Pennsylvania.

Sensors attached to the bat feed data about the swing into a computer. Seconds later, the batprint is generated. The Batronic Bat Swing Analyzer was patented in 1991 by Robert, Thomas, and John Matcovich.

The first swing is slow (0.6 second), looping, and would have very little chance of making contact with a ball. The pro swing is quicker, exploding from zero to nearly 80 mph in 0.3 of a second. Notice the pitch velocities.

In 1994, a California Little League coach patented a device that gives hitters *verbal* feedback. Depending on the swing, a synthesized voice shouts responses such as "Home run!" or "Get focused!"

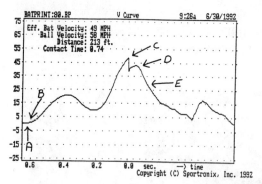

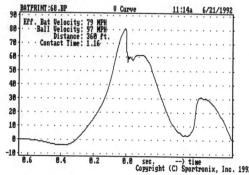

Figures 2-15A,B   *(Sportronix)*

▼ *Figure 2-16* It doesn't matter how fast or pretty a swing is if the hitter doesn't react quickly enough to the pitch. The Sports Technique and Reaction Trainer (START) was originally created for tennis players by former Mets trainer Larry Mayol and Rick Elstein, owner of Syosset Tennis Academy on Long Island.

For baseball training the hitter takes his stance at a double batting tee, which holds balls on the inside and outside corners of the plate. START is positioned on a tripod behind a net. If one light flashes, the hitter has about half a second to swing at an inside fastball. Other cues signal an outside pitch, brushback pitch, or ball outside the strike zone. If the hitter doesn't react quickly enough, a horn blares to indicate the ball would have crossed the plate. The exercise helps the hitter's timing and quickness. Colorado Rockies slugger Howard Johnson has worked extensively with START.

Figure 2-16   *(S.T.A.R.T. Technologies)*

If all else fails, try reading a book.

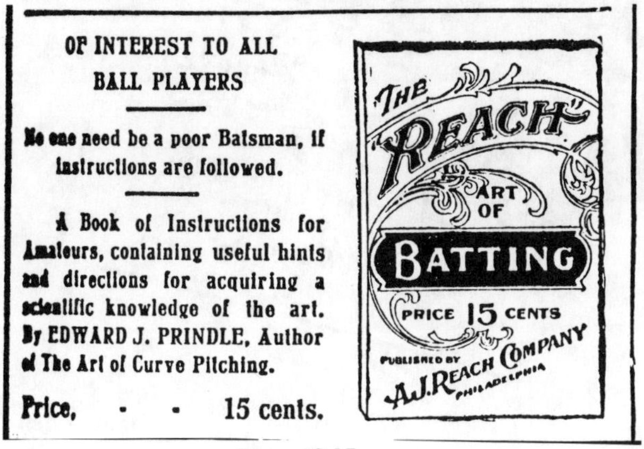

Figure 2-17

PITCHING PRACTICE

▼ **The Artificial Curveball.** *Figures 2-18A, B*   Throwing a curve-ball became almost an obsession among baseball players after the pitch was developed in the 1860s by Hall of Famer Candy Cummings (seen here). An 1886 book titled *The Art of Curve Pitching* was so successful

Figure 2-18A
(Library of Congress)

THE LATEST.
THE
BASE BALL CURVER.
WITH ITS USE ANY PERSON CAN CURVE A
BALL IN ANY DESIRED DIRECTION.
Price 25c. Each.
FOR SALE AT
A. J. REACH & CO.,
1022 MARKET ST., PHILADELPHIA,
AND
RAWLINGS BROS.,
N. E. COR. 8TH AND CHESTNUT STREETS, ST. LOUIS, MO.
Liberal Discount to Dealers.

Figure 2-18B

that author Edward J. Prindle found enough material for a sequel, *The Art of Zigzag Curve Pitching.*

For pitchers who lacked the skill necessary to throw curveballs on their own, a number of inventors (Prindle included) dreamed up devices that would lend them a hand.

The 1888 baseball curver on the left was invented by Alfred Baker and John McKenna of St. Louis. It was a piece of rubber with a loop that was slipped around the second finger. The body of the curver was roughened in order to put added spin on the ball when it was released. "Figure 3" shows the correct position for an "outcurve," "Figure 4" for an "up-shoot," and "Figure 5" for a "down-shoot."

The curver on the right was patented in 1912 by Ralph Jones of Lincoln, Nebraska. It was simply a suction cup wrapped like a ring around the pitcher's first finger. Jones claimed it was for "retarding to a certain extent and in a certain manner the action of the ball when thrown so as to give the same such a movement as to curve when passing through the air."

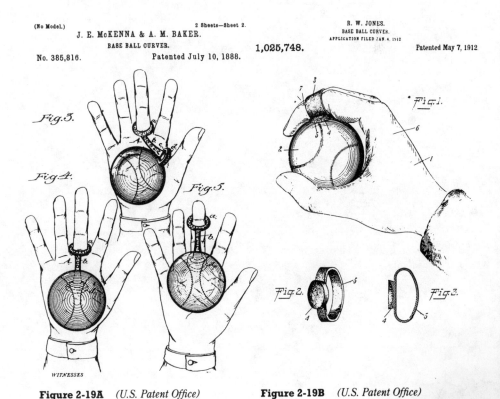

Figure 2-19A *(U.S. Patent Office)*   **Figure 2-19B** *(U.S. Patent Office)*

▼ **The Bionic Pitcher.** *Figure 2-20* Shortly after the invention of the curveball came the invention of the sore arm. To combat this plague, John D. Rafert of Cleveland devised this system of elastic straps and buckles in 1914.

Rafert not only claimed his arm supporter would "relieve the arm from the shock incurred when a ball is suddenly released in the art of throwing," he also promised it would help a pitcher "project the ball with greater speed than he can obtain without its aid." Maybe this is what kept Nolan Ryan going all those years.

▼ **Ball Returners.** *Figures 2-21A, B, C, D* It's not always easy to find a warmup catcher, so inventors set out to design systems that would return the ball to the pitcher automatically for solo practice.

Fred Wood's 1912 "Ball Returning Device" was a simple and elegant—though not exactly portable—solution to the problem. It used the force of the pitch to propel the return throw. If the pitcher hurled the ball into the strike zone–sized opening at the bottom, the ball would whip up around the tunnel and return to him. It was also a clever motivation for learning control. If a pitcher didn't throw strikes, he did a lot of chasing.

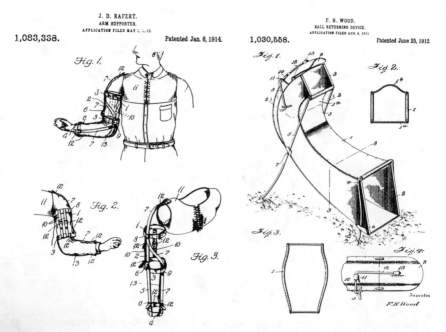

Figure 2-20 *(U.S. Patent Office)*   **Figure 2-21A** *(U.S. Patent Office)*

Harvey Westgate's "Automatic Umpire" of 1916 eliminated that problem. If the ball passed through the opening (24), it was in the strike zone. If it didn't, it was stopped by a wall. The platform and runway were slightly inclined so gravity would send the ball back to the pitcher for his next toss. Westgate, a Los Angeles man, intended the machine to be used mainly as an amusement park game.

John Dean of Yonkers, New York, had a similar idea with his 1921 "Amusement and Exercise Apparatus." Instead of having the ball slam against a wall, Dean used a softer canvas backing (11). The ball was returned to the pitcher via a chute (12).

In 1965, Carl Jackson of Perry, Oklahoma, patented this electric "Target device" made of elastic netting. The net bounced the ball back to the pitcher, and a light or bell would indicate if the pitch was a strike or a ball. Jackson's machine even kept track of the count, with lights on top of the net. After three strikes or four balls were registered, the machine would reset itself automatically. This netting system seems to have survived as the method of choice for pitchers practicing solo.

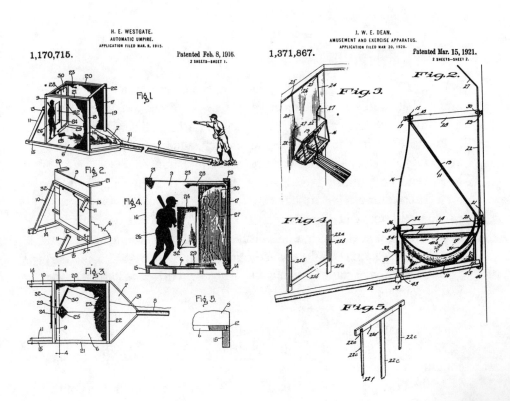

Figure 2-21B *(U.S. Patent Office)*   **Figure 2-21C** *(U.S. Patent Office)*

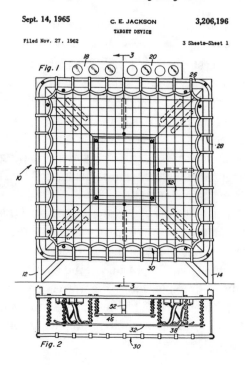

Figure 2-21D   *(U.S. Patent Office)*

▶ **How Fast?** *Figure 2-22*   Despite our admiration for curveball, knuckleball, and screwball specialists, the *fastball* has always been the measure of pitching prowess. The image of a fireballer rearing back, putting every ounce of muscle behind a pitch, and trying to blow away a guy with a stick continues to capture our imagination.

We'll never know for sure who was the fastest pitcher in baseball history. The oldtimers left us before a machine could be developed that would accurately clock their high hard ones. Amos Rusie, who pitched in the 1890s, was so fast that the distance to home plate was increased just so hitters would stand a chance against him.

Bob Feller once said, "The only guy who could throw as hard as I was Walter Johnson."

Walter Johnson said in 1912, "Listen, my friend, there's no man alive can throw harder than Smokey Joe Wood."

Wood (34–5 that season, with 258 strikeouts and a 1.91 ERA) had no comment on the subject.

At the beginning of the century, the fastest trains could go about a hundred miles an hour, so *that* speed became synonymous with "fast." In 1914, Walter Johnson—"The Big Train"—was clocked at 99.7 mph using a primitive ballistic pendulum device. He was in his prime that year, with a 28–18 record and 1.72 ERA.

But it's not likely Johnson could throw a three-digit fastball. "If you look at films of Walter Johnson pitching," says Bill James, "you'll see he threw off his back foot. To me, to throw 100 miles per hour with that motion is just impossible. Most of the pitches in baseball of that era were probably in the range of 75–80 mph." (Most pitches today, it is fair to say, are only 80–84 mph.)

During World War II, it became a publicity stunt for pitchers to throw their fastballs alongside a speeding motorcycle racer. The fans enjoyed the spectacle of man against machine, and pitchers got at least a *rough* gauge of how fast they were throwing.

The war prompted the development of technology that could measure the velocity of a moving object more accurately. A Maryland munitions company developed a device that used photoelectric cells to clock artillery shells. In May 1946, Bob Feller and the Cleveland Indians were in town to play the Washington Senators, so the apparatus was brought in for a demonstration.

Feller, then 27, was considered the fastest in the game. He'd thrown a no-hitter against the Yankees on April 30 and was on his way to a 26-victory, 348-strikeout season. Rapid Robert threw about 40 balls at the machine (seen here), with the fastest one clocked at body temperature—98.6 mph.

Figure 2-22 *(Collection of Bob Feller)*

"The speed at home plate was 98.6 miles an hour and when I released the ball it was 117.2," claims Feller. "They figured the average speed of the ball—and I have movies of it, both sound and silent—and they figured the average speed—which of course I couldn't continue for a whole ball game—was 107.9. Maybe I could sustain 104 miles an hour."

Feller lost the game that day, 2–1 in extra innings. Maybe he used up his best fastballs for the sake of science.

There's no way of knowing if the technology of the day was accurate. Van Lingle Mungo, the Brooklyn Dodgers star from the 1930s, was once clocked at 118 mph at West Point. Minor league legend Steve Dalkowski was clocked at 108 mph in 1962. A softball pitcher named Ty Stofflet rang in at 104.7 mph.

In any case, the machine that was used to clock Feller was impractical. It couldn't be lugged out to the diamond routinely and it couldn't be used during a real game. What was needed was a portable device that tracked the speed of a moving object from a distance.

▼ **The JUGS Gun.**   *Figure 2-23*   In September 1974, Michigan State baseball coach Danny Litwhiler (seen here) was reading the front page of the student newspaper, which had the headline: "Be Careful! Don't Speed on Campus!" Below it was a photo of a campus policeman pointing a newfangled "gun" that was being used to catch speeders in the act.

Figure 2-23

(Collection of

Danny Litwhiler)

"I looked at it and I thought, 'I wonder if that would check a base-ball?'" says Litwhiler.

Daniel Webster Litwhiler had played 11 seasons for the Phillies, Cardinals, Boston Braves, and Cincinnati Reds, hitting .281 lifetime. In 1942, he became the first major league outfielder to play every inning of every game for a season without committing an error. His glove is in the Hall of Fame. After retiring in 1952, Litwhiler became a college coach and invented a variety of devices to help his players (see page 75).

When he saw the notice in the paper, Litwhiler called the campus police and somehow convinced them to come over to the baseball field with a radar gun. The gun was attached to the patrol car and powered by its cigarette lighter.

A Michigan State pitcher was brought over. As he threw baseballs, the officer pointed the gun at him. It registered 75 mph. Litwhiler was thrilled. Curious, he brought the pitcher and police car over to a pitcher's mound and tried it again. This time the gun registered 85 mph. The gun caught about 75 percent of the pitches thrown.

Immediately, Litwhiler wrote to Commissioner Bowie Kuhn about the discovery. "I wanted all the clubs to have the information at the same time," he says, "so one team wouldn't have the advantage over any other." Within a week, he was deluged with requests for more information.

The police radar gun was made by a Colorado company called CMI, Inc., but they saw no future in it for baseball purposes. So Litwhiler contacted John Paulson, inventor of the JUGS pitching machine (see page 53). Paulson was interested, and said he could attach a battery to the gun so it wouldn't be necessary to drive a car out to the field.

A prototype was developed that picked up 99 out of 100 pitches, with an accuracy of plus or minus 1 mph. Litwhiler took it to spring training in 1975 and managers fell in love. "Earl Weaver went crazy with it," says Litwhiler. "He was shooting birds and anything that moved."

The JUGS gun quickly became standard equipment in baseball, and not just to determine bragging rights for the 100-mph club. Generally speaking, a pitcher's curveball should be 15 mph slower than his fastball, his slider 10 mph slower, and his change-up 20 mph slower, regardless of the speed of the fastball. A gun enables a pitching coach to work on these speed differences, as well as to see the effect of a pitcher tinkering with his delivery.

Managers use the gun to determine if a pitcher is running out of gas. Scouts use it to evaluate prospects. Broadcasters use it to bring new information to numbers-hungry fans.

The gun has also been used to clock catchers' throws to second base.

Some of them approach 90 mph (and that's with no windup, from a squat!). Tennis players use it to clock their serves. Andre Agassi and Monica Seles own their own guns.

The only thing the gun has failed to do is calculate the speed of baserunners. Apparently, even the fastest human isn't fast enough to register.

Along with Danny Litwhiler's 1942 glove, his JUGS gun prototype is now in the Hall of Fame. Litwhiler doesn't claim to be its inventor, but more modestly calls it his "discovery."

So who's the fastest in the world? Nolan Ryan was clocked at 100.9 twice during a game on August 20, 1974, in Anaheim Stadium when he was pitching for the Angels. Ryan struck out 19 Detroit Tigers that night, but lost the game in the 11th inning. According to JUGS, only two current players reach the 100-mph barrier—Rob Dibble and Randy Johnson. Johnson, at six-ten and 225 pounds, is almost a freak of nature.

The unfortunate side effect of the speed gun is that scouts and base-ball experts rely on it very heavily in evaluating pitchers. It's hard for a young player to get a chance in the big leagues today if he can't coax an 85- to 90-mph reading out of the gun. It should be remembered that pitchers such as Rudy May and Randy Jones were successful despite the fact that their fastballs never even reached 80 mph.

> *The fastest pitches ever recorded were thrown by Nolan Ryan and Goose Gossage. An All-Star game in St. Louis. Both were clocked at a hundred and three miles per hour. This guy Finch throws sixty miles an hour faster! We thought something was wrong with the measuring gun. But the fact is that it showed a hundred and sixty-eight! You can barely see the ball—just enough of a blur to know that it's not a magic trick.*
>
> (*from* The Curious Case of Sidd Finch, *by George Plimpton*)

▲ **How Does It Work?** The JUGS gun transmits a 10,525-MHz microwave beam, which bounces off the moving baseball and returns. The gun calculates the difference in frequency between the original wave and the reflected wave, then translates this information into miles per hour. The gun works best when the ball is heading toward it or away from it, but it can also work from an angle up to 15 degrees.

When a pitch is clocked at 90 mph, it *doesn't* mean that was the average speed of the pitch. The number represents the speed of the pitch at *one instant in time.* Most pitches slow down about 8 mph on their way to the plate. The newer speed guns can give *two* readings—the first one seven feet from the pitcher's hand and the second one three-quarters of the distance to the plate.

▼ *Figure 2-24.* John Paulson, codeveloper of the JUGS gun, used one during the 1977 World Series.

▲ Recently, a Japanese company named Tsukuda announced "Speed Tracker," a baseball with a built-in semiconductor that calculates velocity. When the ball leaves the pitcher's hand, a switch is activated that trips a timer. When the ball smacks into the catcher's glove, a shock-sensitive switch stops the timer. A tiny window on the ball flashes the speed in miles per hour.

Naturally, the ball can't be used in a game. One hit and it's finished.

▶ **SuperVision.**   *Figure 2-25*   The state of the art in pitch tracking is "SuperVision," a computer imaging system developed by SZL Sport-

Figure 2-24   *(JUGS, Inc.)*

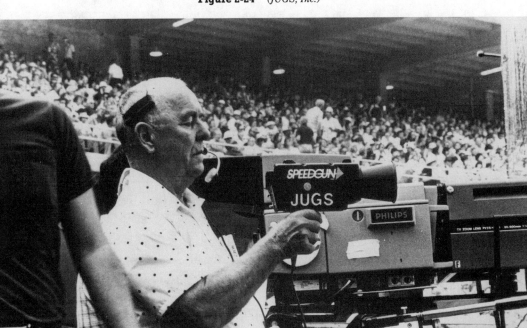

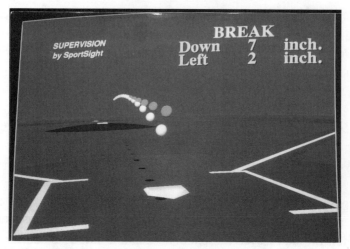

Figure 2-25   *(SportSight, Inc.)*

Sight of Melville, New York. It displays and analyzes the motion of a baseball from the instant it leaves the pitcher's hand until it crosses the plate. Every pitch can be dissected in a way that goes beyond the capabilities of a radar gun. The public saw SuperVision for the first time during the 1990 World Series.

The technology was developed to track missiles for the aerospace industry. Here's how it works: Two video cameras are placed 150 feet up in the left-field stands, at 45-degree angles to each other. They're aimed at the area between the pitcher's mound and home plate. The cameras, which capture images 60 times each second, feed images into two computers.

The analysis is based on the ancient navigational principle of triangulation—using two fixed points to find the location of a third. After each pitch, the computers analyze the slightly different angles from the video cameras and re-create the trajectory of the ball in three dimensions. A computer graphic representation of the batter's strike zone is then superimposed over the real picture, and the precise path of the ball is presented over an instant replay.

By tapping a few keys on the computer, one can view the pitch from above, from behind the plate, from the side, from center field, or even looking up from home plate.

In addition to the actual baseball in flight, the computer also generates the path of an imaginary "reference" ball. This ball shows how the pitch would have moved if it had been influenced only by gravity, *not* by the spin imparted by the pitcher. If the reference ball and the real ball go through the strike zone together, the pitcher doesn't have much movement on his pitches. If the two balls diverge widely on the way to the plate, it means the pitcher has great stuff.

Three seconds after a pitch is thrown, you can see its exact trajectory, the speed in miles per hour at six different points, and how many inches it moved up, down, left, or right. The computer can store every pitch in a game, or every pitch a guy threw last season.

Now *this* is what baseball needs—more statistics!

▼ **Danny Litwhiler: The Thomas Edison of Baseball.** *Figure 2-26A*　The JUGS gun is one of many inventions Danny Litwhiler (seen here) has given to baseball. Here are his other brainstorms.

▼ **Litwhiler's Fly Swatter.** *Figure 2-26B*　Danny noticed that after booting ground balls, infielders usually gave up on them. To force them to scramble after the ball in such situations, in 1958 he designed this flat, pocketless mitt specifically *not* to catch the ball. "I had three of

Figure 2-26B *(Collection of Danny Litwhiler)*

Figure 2-26A *(Collection of Danny Litwhiler)*

them made and they were all stolen," says Litwhiler, "so I guess it was a pretty good idea." Goldsmith-MacGregor made the Fly Swatter for a time, but it is not currently on the market. The photo is Woody Woodward's left arm.

▼ **The Instructional Bunting Bat.**　*Figure 2-26C*　Danny always told his hitters that to bunt correctly, you have to have the *top* half of the ball meet the *bottom* half of the bat. While Litwhiler was coaching Florida State in 1957, a student named Ron Fraser suggested, "Coach, if that's right, why don't you take away the part that's not supposed to hit the ball?" Litwhiler thought that was an excellent idea and had a carpenter carve this bat. It was too light, so he cut a hole in it and filled it with lead. As soon as Casey Stengel saw it, he ordered a dozen. The bat is manufactured by Worth today. Ron Fraser went on to coach the University of Miami and the U.S. Olympic baseball team.

▲ **The Unbreakable Mirror.**　One day in 1961, Danny saw a toothpaste commercial showing bullets bouncing off the front end of an airplane. It made him wonder if a mirror could be built that would withstand the impact of a fastball. That way, a pitcher could throw at the

Figure 2-26C　*(Collection of Danny Litwhiler)*

glass and watch his own delivery. Litwhiler went to the Pittsburgh Plate Glass Company and they designed a 650-pound, five-by-three-foot Herculite mirror that could stand up to a 100-mph fastball. Litwhiler calls it "my instant movie." He used it for 26 years as a college coach and brought it with him when he coached for the Cincinnati Reds in 1983. The Reds still use it today, but the unbreakable mirror is not currently being manufactured.

▼ **The Multiple Batting Cage.** *Figure 2-26D* When you've got 30 hitters on a team, there's never enough time for everybody to get batting practice. While coaching Florida State in 1962 Danny invented this batting cage that could handle as many as five hitters at a time. With a strike zone–sized hole cut in the netting, it encouraged pitchers to throw strikes and batters to hit the ball up the middle. It's the only invention Danny bothered to patent, and JUGS still sells it.

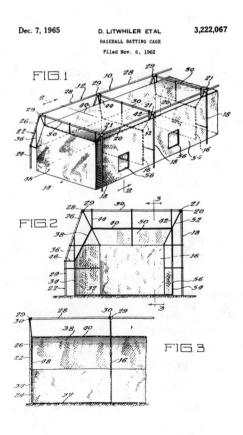

Figure 2-26D *(U.S. Patent Office)*

▲ **Diamond Dust.** In 1956, Danny was at a college football game with his neighbor Jack Moore when it started raining. The referees kept trying to dry the ball with a towel. Moore, a chemical engineer, said there must be a better solution to the problem. Litwhiler said he had the same problem with baseballs on rainy days.

Moore devised a dirt/clay mixture that absorbed water. Danny tested it out by soaking a ball and then rubbing it in the stuff. In 20 seconds, the ball was completely dry. "Diamond Dust," as it came to be called, is now also used with tennis balls and racquets. Danny uses the stuff to soak up oil spills on his driveway.

"Now if you can come up with something to dry a wet field," Litwhiler told Moore, "we'll have something that will save everybody money and time." That led to . . .

▲ **Diamond Grit.** Diamond Dust would be too expensive to spread over an infield, but Moore developed a type of "calcined clay" that absorbed water so quickly that it turned wet mud into dirt in minutes. Each particle of the stuff absorbs more than its own weight in water. Diamond Grit is sold by Floridin Company of Quincy, Florida, and used in ballparks all over the country.

Before Diamond Grit was developed, groundkeepers used to dump sawdust over wet infields, soak it with gasoline, and set the whole thing on fire. If the field was *really* wet, they'd add old tires to the worst spots and burn them. It was terrible for the dirt, and created air pollution. Sometimes helicopters hovered over baseball diamonds to dry them, another waste of gasoline.

▲ **The Heavy Ball.** Practicing with something heavy and then switching to a lighter version at game time is an old sport tradition. Ty Cobb used to put lead weights in his shoes during spring training to make him run faster on Opening Day.

In the late 1960s, Danny figured that training with a heavier-than-normal baseball would increase a pitcher's muscle strength and the velocity of his fastball. He had some balls made with steel ball bearings inside and found that college pitchers throwing them over a 10-week period increased their velocity 14.6 percent with no loss of accuracy (this would have been impossible to measure had Danny not created the JUGS gun first). Worth, Inc., liked the idea and sells a package of five baseballs that weigh 7, 9, 10, 11, and 12 ounces.

Litwhiler also designed a weighted catcher's mitt, which he used to strengthen his players' arms and enhance their quickness. The mitt had a pound of lead wire laced around the fingers. Wilson made it for him but never put it on the market.

▼ **The Lit-Picker.**   *Figure 2-26E*   Danny was coaching for the Cincinnati Reds in 1983. After a long batting-practice session he had to pick up dozens of baseballs, and he was aching all over. That night he dreamed up this gadget that picks up balls without forcing the user to bend down.

▲ **The Can't Release Golf Glove.**   In 1983, Danny noticed that a lot of hitters let go of the bat with their top hand in the middle of the swing, which took away much of their power. So he rigged up a simple device

Figure 2-26E   *(Collection of Danny Litwhiler)*

that used Velcro to make the top hand stick to the bat for the duration of the follow-through. It was never marketed.

Litwhiler has also experimented with swinging a bat underwater, eye patches to encourage hitters to use their dominant eye, and yo-yos to help pitchers throw better curveballs.

"I would try to give the kids something new every year," Litwhiler says. "Players would come to spring training and ask, 'What did you invent over the winter, Danny?' I always figured that if I had something new, the players would think, 'We have something the other teams don't have. We're a little better than they are.'"

Litwhiler is a consultant for JUGS and Worth, but never made an effort to benefit financially from his inventions. His reward comes when he sees someone on TV using a JUGS gun and hears Joe Garagiola (a teammate in 1946) say, "You know, my friend Danny Litwhiler is the guy who came up with that idea."

"You can get into the Hall of Fame even if you aren't a great ballplayer," says Litwhiler. "All you have to do is invent something."

▼ **Thomas Edison, Ballplayer.** *Figure 2-27* The most famous inventor of all time was a baseball fan who would occasionally come out to

Figure 2-27   *(U.S Dept. of the Interior, National Park Service, Edison National Historical Site)*

the ballpark to conduct a few experiments on the mound. *The New York Times* reported on June 21, 1921, that the Wizard of Menlo Park made a relief appearance in a game between his laboratory staff and his Disk Record Department in West Orange, New Jersey.

"After 'winding up' Mr. Edison pitched the first ball, which the batter avoided by ducking, but the fifth ball pitched was near enough the plate to produce a foul. Then the inventor retired to the side lines."

Not a terrific outing, but after all, Edison *was* 74 at the time.

"I was always too busy a boy to indulge in baseball," he remarked. Edison is pictured here laying down a bunt in front of catcher Connie Mack.

OTHER PRACTICE INVENTIONS

▼ **Ball Slinger, 1913.** *Figure 2-28* Here's an alternative to the fungo. "The object . . . is to produce an implement of this character by means of which a ball may be picked up from the ground in the mouth

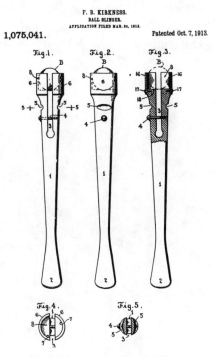

Figure 2-28 *(U.S. Patent Office)*

of the slinger and thrown a great distance by hand, without touching the ball at all," wrote inventor Frederick Kirkness, an Englishman residing in Newark, Delaware. The slinger was made of wood, 24 inches long. A coach would swing it like a bat to sling the ball.

Kirkness had grand visions of his invention. "It is quite possible," he wrote, "that an implement of this character may be used for pitching balls in games of base ball, and in that case a considerable curve could be given to the ball if the player were sufficiently dexterous."

▼ **Bicycle Seat for Catchers.** *Figure 2-29* Here's a great idea. Las Vegas inventor Keith Groves claimed it "lessens the strain on the knees and legs of the catcher and thereby helps the catcher maintain top performance during the game and extends his life as a catcher."

It also comes in handy to block the plate from sliding baserunners. Note the groin protector in the front.

▶ **Slide-Rite.** *Figure 2-30* Slide-Rite was invented by Tom Tresh, the former Yankee and American League Rookie of the Year in 1962. It's a large nylon pad with a canvas sheet on top, which slides when the runner lands on it. According to Tresh, Slide-Rite is used indoors and outdoors by major league, college, high school, and Little League teams. Football and volleyball teams also use it for diving drills.

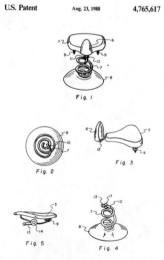

U.S. Patent   Aug. 23, 1988   4,765,617

Fig. 1

Fig. 2   Fig. 3

Fig. 5   Fig. 4

Figure 2-29 *(U.S. Patent Office)*

Figure 2-30 *(Slide-Rite)*

▼ **Heads Up!** *Figure 2-31* In this 1958 photo, Chicago White Sox catchers Earl Battey, Sherm Lollar, and Chuck Lindstrom practice their pop-ups with Air-Flite, a machine that shot baseballs up in the air using air pressure. Coach Tony Cucinello looks on.

Lindstrom, a rookie, is one of the few players in baseball history who had a career batting average of 1.000. He came to the plate twice in 1958. The first time up he walked. In the second at bat he tripled to drive in a run, scored, and that was his career.

Figure 2-31 *(AP/Wide World Photos)*

▼ **Indoor Baseball.**   *Figures 2-32A, B*   In 1887, Chicago reporter George W. Hancock was waiting with friends in the Farragut Boat Club for the results of the Army-Navy football game to come in via telegraph. To kill the time, Hancock took a broomstick for a bat and a boxing glove for a ball and improvised a game of baseball. The indoor game was called "kitten ball" for years, in honor of a team of Minneapolis firemen named "The Kittens." In time, it came to be called softball.

The game was ridiculed as unmanly by some. In 1935, an inmate at Michigan State Prison wrote this poem:

> *Muggsy McGraw looked out from his coffin,*
> *Dead men, you know, don't speak very often,*
> *"Who started Soft Ball, this country to soften?"*
> *Muggsy sighed and he yelled,*
> *He fought and rebelled:*
> *"Why this is a girl's game invented for missies,*
> *What are we coming to—a nation of sissies?"*

Indoor softball is having a revival in the 1990s. Entrepreneurs are turning indoor tennis courts into softball fields and charging teams to play during cold weather months.

Figures 2-32A,B
(Spalding)

3

Around the Ballpark

▶ **Bleachers.** *Figure 3-1* Have you ever stopped and asked yourself why fans sit in "bleachers"? What do bleachers have to do with baseball seats?

Before the turn of the century, ballparks were made of wood. In those old ballparks, just like today, some of the seats were under a roof and others were exposed to the sun. The sun seats, usually less expensive planks in the outfield, became bleached gray over the years. So they came to be called "the bleachers."

It's another romantic story of baseball's simpler past. Unfortunately, those old wooden bleachers had a disturbing tendency to collapse and burn down. Three ballparks went up in flames in 1894 alone. In 1903, 14 people were killed when a grandstand in Philadelphia collapsed.

Technology to the rescue! Steel-framed buildings began going up in the 1890s, ushering in the age of the steel-and-concrete ballpark. In 1909, Shibe Park was built at 21st Street and Lehigh Avenue in Philadelphia. Three months later, Forbes Field opened in Pittsburgh. Boston's Fenway Park and Detroit's Tiger Stadium were completed in 1912. Ebbets Field opened in 1914, Wrigley Field in 1916, and Yankee Stadium in 1923.

Baseball fans rhapsodize about how these old ballparks had quirky, asymmetrical dimensions. It wasn't by design. The automobile had yet

Figure 3-1   *(Hellmuth, Obata & Kassabaum, Inc.)*

to conquer America, so the ballparks were built to fit within inner-city neighborhoods. The fields *had* to be shaped oddly.

After about 50 years, those ballparks began to show their age. Some were preserved (Wrigley, Fenway), others renovated (Yankee), and some destroyed (Shibe, Forbes, Ebbets). By then, most American families had a car, and many used them to flee the crime-ridden cities for the suburbs. The 1960s and 1970s stadiums—no longer called ballparks— were multipurpose, artificial turf–covered, flying saucer–shaped structures ten miles outside town. They featured perfect sight lines, but seats too far away to see much of anything.

Now the tide is turning. Fans have identified 1920–1960 as baseball's "Golden Age." The most exciting new *ballpark* is Baltimore's Camden Yards (seen here), an open-air, baseball-only throwback with just 48,000 seats, odd dimensions, tricky corners, real grass on the field, and advertising on the outfield walls. The ballpark was not only built right in downtown Baltimore, it was built on the site of a saloon owned by Babe Ruth's dad.

Yet Camden Yards is in touch with the 1990s, with diapering facilities in the men's rooms and a JumboTRON video board. The park was designed by the Kansas City architectural firm Hellmuth, Obata, and Kassabaum (HOK), which has designed similar "retro" ballparks for Denver and Cleveland.

▼ **The Eighth Wonder of the World.** *Figure 3-2* The Skydome in Toronto is a compromise between the old and the new. This patent reads, "Covered stadiums are becoming more common because they provide a controlled environment for outdoor sports and extend the season for such activities. However, an indoor atmosphere is a drawback when the weather is fine because it detracts from the natural environment. To obtain the best of both worlds retractable roofs have been devised."

The Skydome's 11,000-ton roof is made of four panels. At the press of a button, two panels slide straight back and a third rotates 180 degrees as it moves on a curved path. In 20 minutes the whole field and 91 percent of the seats are uncovered.

The stadium can change from baseball to football overnight by sliding 18,000 field-level seats along tracks. There's an "acoustical curtaining system" to create an intimate feeling regardless of the attendance. The scoreboard is three stories high by nine stories wide—the largest video display in the world. If the game is a bore, fans can wander around the stadium and find a mall, 18 McDonald's, four restaurants, and a hotel overlooking the field.

▲ Domed stadiums do not guarantee protection against problems with the weather. In April 1986 there was a rain delay *inside* the Metrodome in Minneapolis. A tear had developed in the roof and water was pouring in. During a game in 1990, they had to close the roof of the Toronto Skydome because millions of gnats had invaded the stadium.

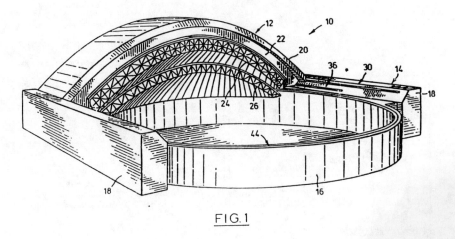

FIG.1

Figure 3-2 *(U.S. Patent Office)*

▼ **The Plate.** *Figures 3-3A, B, C* Home plate started out as a circle, literally a *plate*. It became octagonal in the early 1860s, and then a 12-inch diamond shape in the 1870s. Notice the plate in this 1899 ad for boundary plates.

The problem with a diamond-shaped plate was that umpires had a hard time calling pitches on the outside and inside corners. To correct that problem, home plate was transformed into its current five-sided shape in 1900. So home plate started out looking like a plate . . . but ended up looking like a home. The ad with the modern-looking plate appeared in 1907.

▼ **The Pitching Rubber.** *Figures 3-4A, B* The pitcher's "box plate" in the 1892 ad at left was replaced the following year by a 12-by-4-inch slab we now call the "rubber." The same year, the distance from home plate to the mound was extended to 60 feet 6 inches—which some historians say was the biggest change in the game's history. The pitching rubber continued to be referred to as a "box plate" even after pitcher's boxes were gone, as can be seen from the 1903 ad at right.

Figures 3-3A, B, C
(Sporting Life)

Figures 3-4A, B

▼ **Field Marker, 1909.** *Figure 3-5* "Prior to my invention," wrote Timothy Murname, "it has been the practice to trace the field lines with chalk or lime, either in powdered or liquid form, which in places that are frequently used become quickly obliterated, and may be distinguished for only a short portion of the period of a game." The Boston inventor embedded solid batter's boxes beneath the field, with just the top showing through the dirt.

The idea seems to make sense, but baseball never went for it. Hitters continue to rub out the batter's boxes as early in the game as they can, and the grounds crews keep drawing new ones before every game.

▼ **Where Are Our Inventors?** *Figure 3-6* This 1883 notice cried out for an invention that wouldn't come along for about 100 years. Many

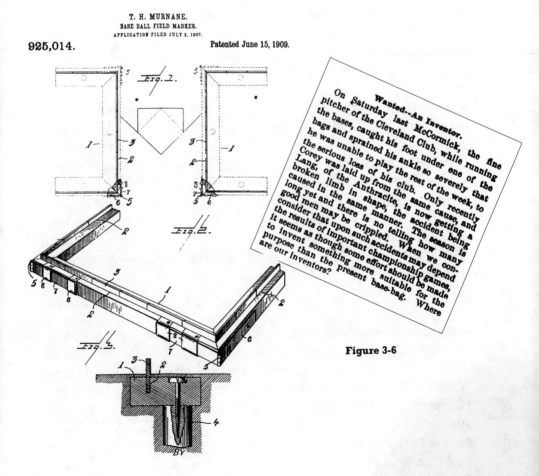

T. H. MURNANE.
BASE BALL FIELD MARKER.
APPLICATION FILED JULY 2, 1907.

925,014.   Patented June 15, 1909.

Fig. 1.

Fig. 2.

Fig. 3.

Figure 3-6

Wanted--An Inventor.

On Saturday last McCormick, the fine pitcher of the Cleveland Club, while running the bases, caught his foot under one of the bags and sprained his ankle so severely that he was unable to play the rest of the week, to the serious loss of his club. Only recently Corey was laid up from the same cause, and Lang, of the Anthracite, is now getting a broken limb in shape, the accident being caused in the same manner. When we consider that upon such accidents may depend the results of important championship games, it seems as though some effort should be made to invent something more suitable for the purpose than the present base-bag. Where are our inventors?

Figure 3-5   *(U.S. Patent Office)*

amateur leagues now use "breakaway bases," which can be pushed out of position by sliding baserunners. In professional baseball, however, bases are simply mounted more securely and players don't often get their feet caught under them.

HELP FOR THE UMPIRE

Umpires have always provided handy authority figures on which to vent our frustration, but many devices have been invented to make their jobs easier—or at least to help them call the game more accurately.

For example, in 1949 somebody designed an "intelligent foul pole." It had swinging rods attached on each side. If a fly ball struck a rod on the foul side, it activated a red light. If it struck a rod on the fair side, it activated a green light. A good idea, but needless to say, umpires are still squinting off into the distance on long shots down the lines, praying they don't blow the call.

▶ **Ding-Dong Base, 1875.** *Figure 3-7* Here's another great idea that never made it—John C. O'Neill's "enunciating base." The St. Louis inventor was awarded a patent for the innovative idea of sticking a bell inside first base. When the runner crossed the bag, the bell would ring.

Wrote O'Neill: "The touching of the base by the runner is clearly announced to the umpire, and the same thereby enabled to render his decision in a perfectly correct and reliable manner, avoiding thereby the dissatisfaction and squabbles arising from erroneous observations and decisions." Unfortunately, the bell rang when the first baseman stepped on the bag too. So we still don't have ringing bases 120 years later.

▶ **Electric Ding-Dong Base.** *Figure 3-8* Another problem with the ding-dong base was that baseball used only one umpire in those days, and he couldn't *hear* the bell from behind the plate. A decade later, William Williams of Huntington, Pennsylvania, came up with a solution. He patented an *electric* version, with the bell placed near home plate and attached to the base by underground wires. But baseball wasn't ready for it in 1885. It still isn't.

Williams was a true baseball visionary. The previous year, he had been issued a patent for a bat made out of paper (see Chapter 1).

J. C. O'NEILL.
BASE-BALL BASE.

No. 171,038.   Patented Dec. 14, 1875.

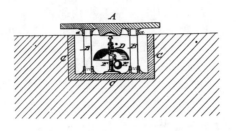

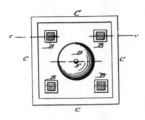

Figure 3-7   *(U.S. Patent Office)*

(No Model.)   2 Sheets—Sheet 2.

W. WILLIAMS.
INDICATOR FOR BASE BALL OR CRICKET FIELDS.

No. 311,278.   Patented Jan. 27, 1885.

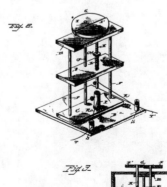

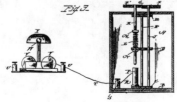

Figure 3-8   *(U.S. Patent Office)*

▲ **Automatic Umpire, 1932.** *Figure 3-9*　There have been a number of attempts to build a machine that would replace the human umpire and his unfortunate tendency to make mistakes. Robert S. Blair of Stamford, Connecticut, invented this elaborate device.

Buried beneath home plate were a motor, an elongated light bulb, lenses, and an electric fan. A thin slot was cut on each side of the plate. Instead of looking at the *ball* as it was delivered, the umpire would look *down.* If he saw the reflection in the mirror of the ball as it crossed the plate, it must have been a strike. If he didn't see the reflection, the pitch must have been out of the strike zone.

Blair's machine had no way of indicating if a pitch was low or high. It would require a second umpire to make that judgment. So instead of eliminating umpires, this machine necessitated using *two* umps behind the plate.

The motor and fan, in case you were wondering, served to blow dust off the lenses.

In the Information Age, where we have instant video and computers

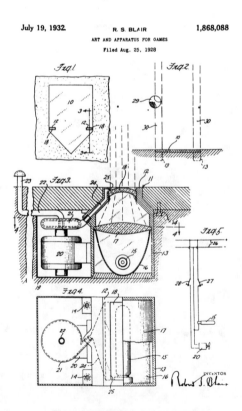

Figure 3-9　*(U.S. Patent Office)*

that can analyze enormous amounts of data, a child could probably design a robot umpire that would never miss a call. In fact, a child already has.

In 1974, 11-year-old Tom Perryman of Dallas built a machine with an energized crystal pumping out sound waves from beneath home plate. A computer calculated how long it took for the waves to bounce off an incoming pitch and return to the crystal.

If it took too long, the pitch had to have been high. Too short, and it was low. Pitches off the inside or outside corner of the plate wouldn't register, and would therefore be called balls.

Ex-ump Ron Luciano tells the story of an automatic umpire that was tested during spring training in the 1970s. This machine used laser beams to sense movement, much like the security systems in stores. Thurman Munson was behind the plate for the demonstration, and the machine kept calling strikes no matter *where* the pitches were thrown.

"Jeez!" Munson yelled to Luciano, "this machine is even blinder than *you!*"

Baseball hasn't actively pursued the idea of automatic umpires, but tennis *has*. In the 1993 U.S. Open, officials used an Australian system with magnetic sensors under the lines, iron particles in the balls, and a computer that searched for flying projectiles every 25-billionths of a second. It's five times more accurate than the sharpest human umpire.

Everyone knows baseball is a very tradition-bound game. But having already violated the traditions of day games, real grass, and even the number of players on each side (with the designated hitter), it's not out of the question that someday the men in blue will become the *machines* in blue.

▲ **Why Do Umpires Use Whisk Brooms?**   Until the turn of the century, umpires cleaned off home plate with a regular long-handled broom. When they were through, they'd toss the broom aside. But during a game in 1904, Jack McCarthy of the Chicago Clubs was running home and tripped over the broom after he crossed the plate. McCarthy damaged his ankle on the play. Soon after, it was ruled that umpires would dust off home plate with a whisk broom and store it in their pocket when not in use.

▶ **Indicators.**   *Figures 3-10A, B, C*   Before the advent of elaborate scoreboards, indicators were sold to fans as well as umpires to keep

Figure 3-10A,B

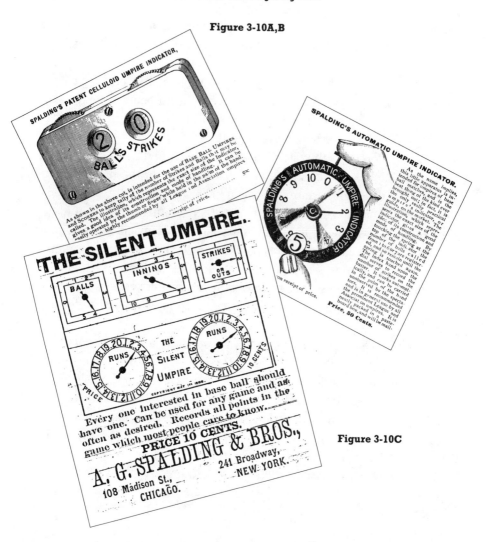

Figure 3-10C

track of the game. Note that Spalding's Automatic Umpire Indicator (1880) records up to seven balls and "The Silent Umpire" (1888) records five. It wasn't until 1889 that batters walked after four pitches out of the strike zone. Spalding's modern-looking "Patent Celluloid Umpire Indicator" premiered in 1887.

▶ *Figure 3-11* In 1890, Frank Collyer of Brooklyn, New York, patented this "score keeper." He wrote: "In the example of my improvement shown I cause the score to be kept for both clubs contesting the game, for runs, outs, innings, errors, and base-hits."

(No Model.)

F. COLLYER.
BASE BALL SCORE KEEPER.

No. 423,027.   Patented Mar. 11, 1890.

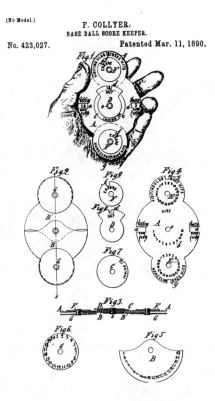

Figure 3-11   *(U.S. Patent Office)*

▶ **Artificial Turf.**   *Figure 3-12*   "If cows don't eat it, I ain't playing on it," Dick Allen used to say. "It would be best if artificial turf would pack up and move to South Yemen," according to Bill James.

Probably the most despised of all baseball inventions, artificial turf was born in the early 1960s after a Ford Foundation study found kids in rural areas were in better physical condition than city kids. From this, a genius at the government's Educational Facilities Laboratory leaped to the conclusion that playing sports on asphalt was detrimental to a growing body's health. The EFL invited corporations to develop an artificial surface that resembled grass, with the idea of putting it in urban playgrounds.

Chemstrand, a division of Monsanto, had been experimenting with an artificial surface called "ChemGrass." It was made of nylon knitted fiber woven into a polyester backing and described as having "the same texture as a stiff, thickly bristled nylon hairbrush." (This was according to Chemstrand, *not* critics.) Monsanto outfitted an indoor fieldhouse at

'Flying Saucer' Stadium in Texas Nearly Ready

Translucent plastic dome covers Harris County Stadium, 20 minutes from downtown Houston. The $20.5 million air-conditioned arena will seat about 46,000 for baseball.

By JOSEPH DURSO

Special to The New York Times

HOUSTON.

Ten architectural and engineering concerns were needed to build it, the Duke of Windsor marveled at it and the New York Yankees will officially open it—the world's first air-conditioned all-purpose stadium with a roof.

Less than 90 days from "launch," the huge Astrodome Stadium here stands nearly finished on the Gulf Coast plain like some weird laboratory of the Government's nearby space center.

It covers nine and a half acres, with 250 more for parking and exhibition space; it cost $3 million for the land

Dome-Covered Building in Houston Will Be Opened by Astros and Yankees

alone, $20.5 million for the stadium itself and $8 million for access roads and parking.

It will draw 250,000 cubic feet of fresh air, process it through 6,600 tons of cooling capacity and then circulate 2.5 million cubic feet—temperature-controlled and humidity-controlled—every minute.

Yet, says Herman Lloyd of the architectural firm of Lloyd, Morgan & Jones, the chief problems in designing this combination sports-convention facility,

unmatched anywhere in the world, were, first, the ability to span 642 feet with a dome; second, the ability to grow grass in an enclosed, air-conditioned stadium, and third, the ability to move 10,000 seats to handle different types of events.

All of these problems have long since been solved, and even the Tiffany Bermuda grass grown at the Texas A. & M. Experimental Station will have been landscaped into the outfield by April 9, when the Yankees open a weekend exhibition series with the Houston Astros and the St. Louis Cardinals to unveil the park.

The whole thing, from cellar to dome, is owned by Harris Continued on Page 4, Column 1

Figure 3-12   *(New York Times)*

Moses Brown School in Providence, Rhode Island, with ChemGrass, making it the first grassy area in the world that didn't have any grass.

The story picks up on April 9, 1965, a date that will live in infamy to baseball purists. The first indoor, air-conditioned baseball game took place that day in Houston's $20-million Astrodome (actually "Harris County Stadium"). Mickey Mantle, in a rear leadoff slot, pasted a single on the second pitch of the exhibition game, and he slammed the first indoor home run a few innings later.

The idea for the Astrodome was hatched in the 1950s when Astro owner Judge Roy Hofheinz worked with futurist and geodesic dome inventor Buckminster Fuller on a domed shopping center. After a trip to Rome in which he learned that the Colosseum had been covered with an awning in A.D. 80, Hofheinz decided a domed stadium would work just fine in Texas.

When the Astrodome was built it had natural grass, not turf. But during the first few games there, outfielders found it so hard to follow the flight of fly balls that they took to wearing batting helmets in the field. The only solution was to paint over the 4,596 Lucite panels in the roof.

Within days, the grass below turned a sickly brown. The groundskeepers tried fertilizing and even *painting* the grass green, but it was hopeless. The natural grass died, and with it an era of baseball.

ChemGrass, as it turned out, was too expensive for urban playgrounds. But it wasn't too expensive for Judge Roy Hofheinz. He came across an article about it and paid $575,000 for ChemGrass to be installed in the Astrodome. It was the media that dubbed it "AstroTurf."

Following the Astrodome, other domed stadiums were built—symmetrical, "cookie-cutter" arenas that could host baseball, football, and rock concerts, though none of them particularly well. By 1977, 11 major league fields were covered with turf. A game born and raised on cow pastures was being played—a good part of the time—on plastic rugs.

Baseball is so different on turf that columnist Russell Baker suggested the major leagues be split into "grassball" and "rugball" divisions. On turf, speed in the field and on the basepaths becomes more important than power at the plate. Lumbering outfielders become real liabilities. Even speedy outfielders play more tenatively because the ball bounces so high off the rug. Infielders are more daring because they know the ball will bounce true, and because few hitters can drop down a soft bunt on the carpet.

Shortstops *intentionally* bounce long pegs to first instead of making the old high-arching throws, because they know the ball will get there faster (an innovation credited to Cincinnati's Dave Concepcion). Some catchers throw intentional short hops to second to catch base stealers.

Runners can't score from second on a single easily, because the ball gets to the outfield so quickly. But hard-hit singles between two outfielders scoot all the way to the wall for doubles.

Artificial turf is *good* for baseball, claim its advocates. It has made the game faster, more aggressive, and more exciting. Turf can withstand up to 80 times more use than grass. It's 10 times cheaper to maintain. It drains water more quickly.

Despite all these advantages of artificial turf, there remains the widespread feeling that the game played on it has one big problem—it just isn't baseball.

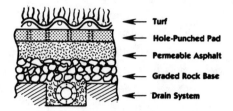

Figure 3-13   *(Balsam Corp.)*

▲ *Figure 3-13*   AstroTurf is made of four layers. The top layer is the turf, which is made of half-inch nylon fibers woven together like a rug. These fibers are crinkled because the original straight AstroTurf fibers tended to flatten out. The next layer is a five-eighths-inch foam rubber pad with holes in it for drainage. Below that is a three-inch layer of permeable asphalt subbase. Finally, a six- to eight-inch layer of loose gravel sits on the bottom. Three-inch pipes under the turf carry water away from the field. AstroTurf has to be replaced every eight years or so, because the padding becomes hardened.

▲ **Turf Facts.**   The first World Series game played on turf took place on October 10, 1970, in Cincinnati between the Reds and the Baltimore Orioles. The St. Louis Cardinals and Minnesota Twins played the first indoor World Series game on October 17, 1987, in Minnesota. The largest concentration of AstroTurf fields is in New York City, where there are 25. The largest indoor stadium with AstroTurf is the Superdome in New Orleans—164,600 square feet. Several companies make turf, but AstroTurf has 60 percent of the market. In 1988, Monsanto sold its AstroTurf division to Balsam Sportstattenbau, a German company.

▶ **Tarpaulins.**   *Figure 3-14*   Tarps came into use around 1910 to protect baseball fields from water. Just three years later, William McDonald of Pittsburgh patented this device, which rolled and unrolled the tarp like a window shade.

The first tarps were made from canvas, sometimes waterproofed with tar, paint, or wax. They still absorbed water, making them heavy and hard to handle. The Cleveland Indians began using a lighter, spun-glass tarp in the 1940s. Today, most teams with grass fields use a nylon tarp, but even that weighs over 1,000 pounds.

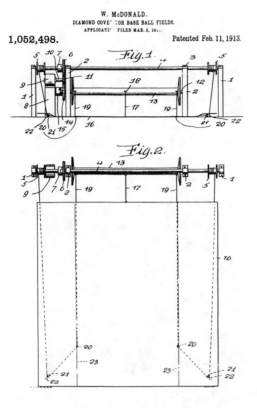

W. McDONALD.
DIAMOND COVE~ ~OR BASE BALL FIELDS.
APPLICATI~ FILED MAR. 3, 19..

1,052,498.

Patented Feb. 11, 1913.

Figure 3-14 *(U.S. Patent Office)*

The strangest tarp incident occurred during the 1985 NLCS when a motorized tarp rammed into Vince Coleman of the St. Louis Cardinals, injuring his leg.

▶ **Fences.** *Figure 3-15* When he owned the minor league Milwaukee Brewers in 1942, Bill Veeck (next page) erected a 60-foot chicken wire fence in right field at Borchert Field. The fence was connected to a hydraulic motor, which could move it into foul territory at the push of a button.

Veeck would move the fence on and off the field between innings, depending on who was hitting. If the Brewers were facing a team with a bunch of lefthanded power hitters, the fence went up and turned their homers into doubles. When the weak-hitting Brewers came to the plate, Veeck slid the fence into foul territory.

In dead-ball days, when home runs were rare, ballparks didn't even

Figure 3-15   *(George Brace)*

have fences. It was Bill Cammeyer, the business manager of the New York Mutuals, who first thought of putting a fence around the outfield in 1862. He did it so he could keep fans *away* from the ballpark and charge admission to the grounds.

Padded fences, a recent innovation, have reduced the number of injuries to outfielders. They have also made the game more exciting, because outfielders are more willing to take chances at making spectacular catches at the wall.

▶ *Figure 3-16*   As far back as 1885, baseball labored under the misconception that fans want seat cushions. Seat cushions *do,* however, make excellent Frisbee substitutes.

▶ **Turnstiles.**   *Figure 3-17*   According to sportscaster Bill Mazer, who was probably there, turnstiles were first used in Providence in 1878 for a game against Boston. Six thousand fans pushed through, and Boston won 1–0.

Figure 3-16

GRAND STAND CUSHIONS FOR BASE BALL GROUNDS.

The Chicago Club have for several seasons furnished cushions to ther patrons at a nominal rental of 5 cents per game. It is a feature highly appreciated by base ball spectators. We are now manufacturing these cushions, and can supply them to clubs at 50 cents each. Special prices made when ordered in hundred lots.

A. G. SPALDING & BROS

241

108 Madison Street,
CHICAGO.

BRIGHT'S AUTOMATIC REGISTERING TURN STILE.

Is acknowledged to be the most reliable, durable and simple Turn Stile made. It is designed especially for Base Ball and Fair Grounds, Expositions, etc., and is an almost indispensable assistant in making a correct division of receipts and avoiding all possibility of the gate-keeper's appropriating any portion of them, by accurately counting and registering each person passing through it.

The movement registers from 1 to 10,000, and can easily and almost instantly be reversed to zero by any person having the key, without the Stile being securely attached and is shipped complete, and used without delay.

necessity of removing from the Stile to which it is locked. It is provided with all necessary stops, etc., to prevent its getting out of order through being handled by meddlesome persons, and is shipped complete and in readiness to be placed beside a doorway or other suitable entrance to inclosure, either permanent or temporary, and used without delay.

They have been in use during the past season by the Cleveland and Philadelphia League Clubs and by all of the Clubs of the N. W. League, without an instance of failure or dissatisfaction, but have since been greatly improved by the addition of several valuable features, making it unquestionably the best adapted and most durable Turn Stile in the market.

Orders from Base Ball Clubs should be sent in as early as possible, insuring their being filled before the beginning of the season.

Price complete..$50 00

Figure 3-17

▲ The first major league team to fly in an airplane was the Boston Red Sox, who flew from St. Louis to Chicago on July 30, 1936.

▲ The first baseball player to be paid to endorse a product was St. Louis Browns first baseman Charlie Comiskey. In 1887 Comiskey hawked a medication called Menell's Penetrating Oil. He would later become a manager, and in 1900 Comiskey bought the Chicago White Stockings. It is Comiskey who often receives blame for the Black Sox Scandal. He vastly underpaid his players, and in 1919 eight of them conspired to throw the World Series in exchange for money from gamblers.

BIRTH OF THE NIGHT GAME

Thursday, September 2, 1880. It was just a year after Thomas Edison invented the incandescent lamp. That evening employees of two Boston department stores, Jordan Marsh and R. H. White, gathered on a field in Hull, Massachusetts, to play the first baseball game under artificial light.

That first night game was a stunt on the part of Boston's Northern Electric Light Company to prove it could illuminate large areas. Three wooden towers were erected around the field, with 12 electric lamps pumping 30,000 candlepower. Two engines and three generators were installed on the side of the field in a small shed.

"When the lamps were lighted after dark the effect was fine," reported *The Boston Post*. "A clear, pure, bright light was produced, very strong and yet very pleasant to the sight."

Three hundred fans watched as the Marsh and White teams battled through nine innings. With the score tied at 16–16, the first night game was called—on account of the last ferry back to Boston.

Baseball was meant to be played during the day, claim baseball purists, not at 10:00 P.M. in some geodesic dome on fake grass with a bunch of prima donna designated hitters. The only problem is, most people go to school or work during the day. Before there were night games, baseball was best observed by the unemployed, the ridiculously wealthy, and others with lots of time to kill.

So inventors set out to design a practical lighting system for night ball. Not all were practical. Common sense suggested putting powerful lights on towers pointing down on the field. But Thomas Edison's Edison Electric Light Company believed such a method would cause harsh shadows and glare in player's eyes.

Instead, Edison's men devised a scheme in which electric lights were buried in the *ground* just outside the foul lines pointing *upward* through corrugated glass. Supposedly, a softer, diffused light would be reflected downward by "atmospheric influences."

"The effect was marvelous," one reporter wrote of a demonstration on Staten Island in 1887. "The ball glistened like a meteor and was, for that reason, more distinct than is usual in the natural light." Thomas Edison was impressed, but never got involved with night baseball himself.

▼ *Figures 3-18A, B, C, D*   When did night baseball first become feasible? Take your pick from (clockwise) 1887, 1910, 1930, and 1935.

▼ *Figure 3-19*   An 1883 night game.

Figures 3-18A,B,C,D
(Author's collection)

REDS' NIGHT GAME DRAWS 25,000 FANS

Many Notables See Contest, First Under Lights in History of Major Leagues.

CINCINNATI BEATS PHILS

Wins, 2-1, Behind Derringer— Sparkling Plays Are Seen in Errorless Battle.

BALL AT NIGHT

ONCE MORE PROVEN ABSOLUTELY FEASIBLE.

With the Proper Plant at the New White Sox Park, Inventor Cahill Convincingly Demonstrates His Lighting Theory as Practical.

SOLVED AT LAST.

Play by Electric Light Possible.

The Scheme to be Again Tried at Staten Island—Difficulties Overcome.

NIGHT BASE BALL PROVES FEASIBLE

Success in Western League Tilt From Lighting and Money Standpoint.

QUITE A SUCCESS.

Base Ball Played at Night by Aid of Electric Lights.

Correspondence SPORTING LIFE.

FORT WAYNE, Ind., June 5.—The game of base ball, between the Quincys, of Illinois, and a picked nine of Fort Wayne players, by electric light, took place last Saturday evening. The inclosure, which is four hundred and seventeen of the lamps of the Jenney Electric Light Company, of Fort Wayne. They were attached to the masts, except three that were suspended as the lights was four hundred and fifty feet, was lighted by the lights up the diamond splendidly, seemed to light at the corner made it light enough to see the ball plainly in the center field. The atmosphere was heavy at times, which caused a very noticeable and favorable effect on throwing the light down on the field. All the lights had a powerful reflector behind them. The only thing to mar the exhibition was the light going entirely out twice, caused by defective brushes at the power-house. It was found necessary to change the ball quite often. When a ball became dirty, it could not be seen. With between twenty-five and thirty lights there is no question but what electric light ball playing is an assured success. Another exhibition game, in a short time. The game was unimportant, as far as the score was concerned and some trouble was experienced in catching the ball from the bat, particularly the high ones but not the least difficulty was found at the bat. But seven innings were played. Quincy winning by 19 to 11. The playing was between the pitcher and catcher, who were enabled to work fairly, owing to the insufficient number of lights used. The out-fielding was unsatisfactory. The grounds were crowded with spectators, whose interest was centered more on the effect the lights had on the flying ball than on the game itself.

Figure 3-19
(Author's collection)

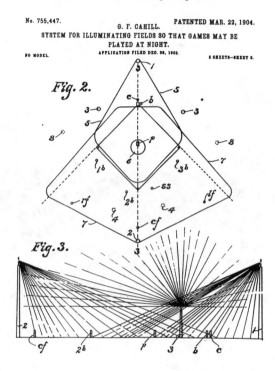

No. 755,447.   PATENTED MAR. 22, 1904.
                                    G. F. CAHILL.
SYSTEM FOR ILLUMINATING FIELDS SO THAT GAMES MAY BE
                           PLAYED AT NIGHT.
NO MODEL.   APPLICATION FILED DEC. 26, 1902.   6 SHEETS—SHEET 2.

Figure 3-20   *(U.S. Patent Office)*

▲ *Figure 3-20*   George Cahill of Holyoke, Massachusetts, patented this portable lighting system and successfully staged a game on the night of June 19, 1909. Three thousand spectators showed up to watch two Cincinnati Elks lodges play. A year later, Cahill put on a demonstration for White Sox owner Charles Comiskey that attracted 20,000 fans.

"Almost 2,000,000 candle power were turned on, with the result that night became as day under their powerful glare," wrote *Sporting Life*. Comiskey was said to be interested, but nothing came of it.

The major leagues ignored night baseball for 30 years. The minor leagues and Negro League, however, took to it in a big way during the Depression. Teams began playing under lights regularly in 1930, with attendance sometimes tripling.

▶ **The First Major League Night Game.**   *Figure 3-21*   Baseball finally gave in. At the National League meeting in 1934, the financially troubled Cincinnati Reds were given permission to play seven night games in 1935, one against each of the other teams in the league. The first major league night game (seen here) took place on May 24, 1935, in Cincinnati: 20,422 fans turned out. Fireworks were exploded, Franklin Delano Roosevelt pushed a button in the White House, and 632 lamps flooded Crosley Field with light.

Paul Derringer of the Reds threw a six-hitter that night, and Cincinnati defeated the Philadephia Phillies 2–1. No errors were made, though two catchable fly balls dropped untouched. The game was broadcast over four radio stations.

"Night baseball is a passing attraction which will not live long enough to make it wise for the New York Club to spend $250,000 on a lighting system," New York Yankee chief Ed Barrow said shortly after the first night game.

The other club owners quickly erected lights in their ballparks. By 1940, most major league parks had lights. Even the Yankees knuckled under in 1946. The last holdout, Wrigley Field, held its first night game on August 8, 1988.

Night baseball not only attracted more fans to the ballpark than day

Figure 3-21   *(AP/Wide World Photos)*

games, it also attracted a larger radio and television audience. Higher ratings translate into more commercial revenue. The powers that be in baseball were never ones to turn down an easy buck, and the game made its inevitable transformation into an evening sport.

The All-Star Game was played at night for the first time in 1942. The World Series held out until 1971. In 1985, *all* games of the World Series were played at night for the first time. A crucial, exciting postseason game now attracts more than 80 million TV viewers.

Typically, kids develop their lifelong love of baseball around the age of eight. The question is whether those kids—the *next* generation of potential fans—will flock to a sport that starts its showcase event after parents shut the bedroom door and say, "Lights *out*."

GETTING THE WORD OUT

▶ *Figure 3-22*   From carrier pigeons to computers, the communications technology of the day has been exploited to get fans the scores, the stories, and the interviews, and finally to experience the game of baseball itself. This clip appeared in an 1883 newspaper.

▶ *Figures 3-23A, B, C*   Most newspapers didn't have a sports section in the 1800s. Sports were considered beneath the dignity of serious-minded readers. There was no radio or television either, so magazines sprang up to supply information to a baseball-starved public.

Beginning in 1876, pitcher/entrepreneur Albert Spalding published his yearly *Spalding Guide,* which contained articles, rule changes, and of course, ads for Spalding sporting goods. Alfred H. Spink sold his first issue of *The Sporting News* on March 17, 1886. It remained in the Spink family until 1977, when it was sold to Times Mirror. *Sporting Life* was born in 1883, and *Baseball Magazine* in 1908.

▶ *Figures 3-25A, B*   When baseball was in its infancy, the problem wasn't getting information to the general public—it was getting information to the people in the *ballpark.* Players' uniforms didn't have names or numbers on them. Scoreboards were primitive, and some parks didn't have one at all. The rules were changing every year, and the fundamentals of

CARRIER PIGEONS IN BASE BALL.

How the Winged Messengers are Utilized to Carry the News.

"Here he comes; we'll know how it went in a minute," exclaimed one of the keepers out at the Philadelphia Zoological Garden Wednesday afternoon to another, as they lounged on the rail by one of seal tanks, and almost while he spoke a homing pigeon flashed across the Schuylkill and an instant later reached its coop on the top of the deer-house. The first speaker captured the bird, and took from one of its legs a little slip of paper. "All O. K.; 6 to 2; the Mets, got one in their last inning" read the message.

"The bird belongs to James Murray, the keeper in charge of the deer-house," said the man in answer to an inquiry from a bystander. "Murray has twenty of them, and sends some over to almost every match played on the Athletic or Philadelphia grounds, and, as it only takes about two minutes for the birds to come home, we keep posted right up to time and can know how an inning went before the next one. Murray has had the birds for about two years, but this is the first season they have been used to bring messages to the Zoo."

Pigeons are also sent from the base ball grounds to other places about the city, and on some days as many as half a dozen birds will be released at the end of an inning.

Figure 3-22 *(Author's collection)*

PRICE 10 CENTS.

SPALDING'S OFFICIAL BASE BALL GUIDE

1884.

PUBLISHED BY

A. G. SPALDING & BROS.,
108 Madison St., Chicago, Ill.

Figure 3-23B *(The Sporting News)*

Figure 3-23C *(Spalding's Official Base Ball Guide)*

Figure 3-24   *(Baseball Magazine)*

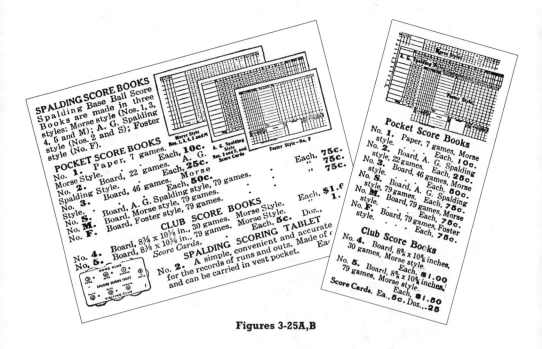

Figures 3-25A,B

the game were not yet a part of the national consciousness. Many fans watching a game had no idea what was going on.

The first scorecard was printed on October 11, 1866, for a game between the Atlantics and Athletics, in Brooklyn. The attendance was said to be 30,000. Henry "The Father of Baseball" Chadwick wrote the first box score in 1859 to encapsulate a game between the Stars and Excelsiors, also in Brooklyn.

▼ **The Megaphone Men.**   *Figures 3-26A, B*   Before 1901, it was the umpire's job to turn around and shout the names of the batteries for the fans and boys in the press box. It was difficult to hear, especially with a noisy crowd. That season, a one-armed Washington scorecard salesman named E. Lawrence Phillips began roaming the stands with a megaphone, which he used to bark out the names of the players, umpires, and pinch-hitters and other helpful information. Soon megaphone men began appearing at other ballparks. This illustration depicts the Baker Bowl in Philadelphia.

The following anecdote has been told about Wrigley Field's Pat Piper, Ebbets Field's Tex Rickard, and just about every other megaphone man: Before one game a group of fans hung their coats over a railing in fair territory. The umpire felt the coats might interfere with the game, so the megaphone man grabbed his megaphone and boomed, "Attention please! Will the fans along the left-field railing please remove their clothing?"

Figure 3-26B   *(New York Times)*

Giants' Amplifying Set Makes Umpire's Voice Audible to All

One of the most interesting features at the Polo Grounds yesterday was the operation of the Giants' newly installed amplifying set, which not only broadcasts the batteries and substitution of players but which enables the umpire to call out each ball and strike so all may hear. This he does by standing on two plates behind the catcher and talking into a microphone attached inside his mask.

To Charlie Rigler fell the lot of introducing the innovation to the fans and even the players had to admit that Charlie had an excellent voice, though as usual they did not always agree with his decisions.

Figure 3-26A   *(Collection of Rich Westcott)*

E. Lawrence Phillips megaphoned Washington Senators games until 1928. The next season was the beginning of the end of the megaphone man era—the electric public address system was introduced at the Polo Grounds.

The St. Louis Cardinals were still using a megaphone man during the Gashouse Gang days of 1934, but eventually amplification took over.

▼ **The First Electric Scoreboard, 1909.** *Figure 3-27* George Baird of Chicago wrote that his invention was "designed more especially for use at a ball-ground or field for the purpose of signaling to all portions, near and far, of an assembled audience the important facts of a game of base-ball, such for instance as the identity of the successive batters, and the different events such as balls, strikes, outs, etc., as they occur in the progress of the game." Before Baird's invention, scoreboards all used large cards with numbers on them and indicated only the inning-by-inning line score of the game.

Figure 3-27   *(U.S. Patent Office)*

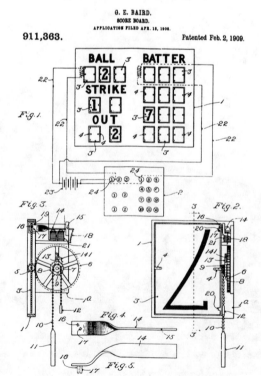

G. E. BAIRD.
SCORE BOARD.
APPLICATION FILED APR. 15, 1908.

911,363.

Patented Feb. 2, 1909.

Electric scoreboards caught on, and when solenoid relays and micro-processors became available, stadiums strove to outdo each other with flashy and increasingly ridiculous displays. The "exploding scoreboard" debuted in Chicago in 1960. Royals Stadium in Kansas City has a "Water Spectacular" show beyond the outfield fence, complete with music and colored lights. Clubs spend millions of dollars so fans can enjoy computer-generated "Dot Races" between innings. Now, *that's* baseball!

Purists prefer the old number cards still used at Fenway Park. But with instant replay on the DiamondVision, being at the ballpark is almost as good as if you were sitting in your living room watching the game on TV!

▼ *Figures 3-28A, B*   Inside the Yankee Stadium scoreboard, before and after it went electric in 1950. That's Jeff Ingenito pulling the weights in the "before" photo, and Benjamin Weiss flipping the switches in the "after."

Figure 3-28A   *(National Baseball Library, Cooperstown, NY)*

Figure 3-28B   *(National Baseball Library, Cooperstown, NY)*

▶ **Telegraphic Baseball.**   *Figure 3-29*   Long before radio became available to the public, the telegraph was used to bring baseball beyond the ballpark. The first game transmitted by telegraph was sent by Harry M. Millar, a reporter for the *Cincinnati Commercial.* Millar followed the Cincinnati Red Stockings on the road in 1869 and sent instant reports back to his readers. This ad appeared in *Sporting Life* in 1886.

▶ *Figure 3-30*   By 1890, telegraph wires had reached most major league ballparks. Saloons and poolhalls would receive scores by telegraph and post them on a blackboard for their customers. This feature would be advertised to draw a crowd, just as today's sports bars hype *Monday Night Football.*

Telegraphed baseball would show up in unusual places. An opera house in Atlanta received game details by telegraph, and performers *acted out* the game on stage. This photo was taken at a Los Angeles railroad station.

In the nineteenth century, as today, teams sold the rights to broadcast their games. Telegraph companies paid in free telegrams, about $300 worth in 1897. And just like today, complaints were heard that broadcasts of baseball would cut down on attendance. "Why should people come out to the ballpark," the owners asked, "when they can enjoy

Figure 3-29   *(Sporting Life)*

BASE BALL Detailed by Telegraph!

MORGAN & CO.,

Of Nashville, Tenn.,

WILL GIVE THEIR "IMPROVED AND PATENTED"

BASE BALL EXHIBITIONS

Commencing in APRIL at CINCINNATI and CHICAGO.

Every Move of the Player Accurately and Graphically Given. Every Game Of the Absent Home Club Reported.

OPEN IN NEW YORK IN MAY.

Figure 3-30   *(National Baseball Library, Cooperstown, NY)*

the game for free in a local bar?" For a time, Charlie Comiskey banned telegraphers from his Chicago park.

But from telegraph to radio to television, technology has always served to make *new* fans and generate interest in baseball, which pays off at the gate.

▲ **The Vibrathrob.**   In 1898, Cincinnati shortstop Tommy Corcoran tripped over a wire while rounding third during a game in Philadephia. He began pulling up the wire and found it led to a perch beyond the outfield fence, where Philadelphia backup catcher Morgan Murphy was sitting with binoculars.

Murphy would steal signs from the opposing catcher and relay them by telegraph to a "vibrathrob" in the coach's box. One tap for a fastball, two for a curve, and three for a change. The coach would then relay the sign to the batter.

▼ **Telegraph Simulations.** *Figures 3-31A, B* In an effort to add realism to telegraphic baseball, boards such as this one by James Cutler of Piketon, Ohio, were designed that roughly simulated the game. Newspapers would set them up in front of their offices as a promotional device, especially during the World Series.

Typically, the board was green with the layout of a diamond on it. An oversized baseball was positioned at the pitcher's position. As the ticker in the newspaper office tapped out the play-by-play, the ball would be lowered straight toward the plate.

If a message was received that the pitch was hit in fair territory, a white square would move around the baselines, indicating where the

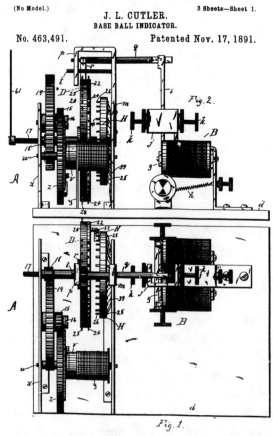

Figure 3-31A   *(U.S. Patent Office)*

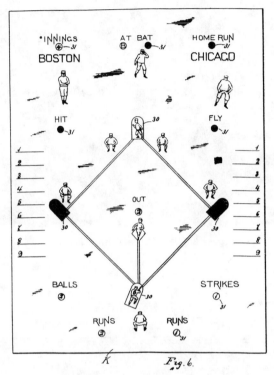

(No Model.)

J. L. CUTLER.
BASE BALL INDICATOR.

No. 463,491.

3 Sheets—Sheet 3.

Patented Nov. 17, 1891.

Figure 3-31B   *(U.S. Patent Office)*

batter ran. If he was called out, the square would return to home plate. The ball was then raised back up to the mound for the next pitch. Balls, strikes, outs, and other details were also registered.

▶ *Figures 3-32A, B, C, D* New York City became a madhouse every year during the World Series. The streets around Times Square became choked off when thousands of people elbowed for position to "see" the game on the New York Times Building indicator board.

These ads appeared during the 1912 World Series, when the Boston Red Sox beat the New York Giants with a run in the tenth inning of the final game. The photo was taken during a game in the 1919 World Series, when the Chicago White Sox threw the Series for gamblers.

Figure 3-32A   *(AP/Wide World Photos)*

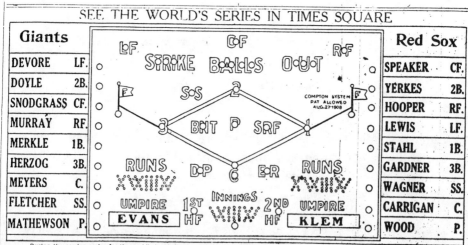

SEE THE WORLD'S SERIES IN TIMES SQUARE

Giants				Red Sox
DEVORE	LF.		SPEAKER	CF.
DOYLE	2B.		YERKES	2B.
SNODGRASS	CF.		HOOPER	RF.
MURRAY	RF.		LEWIS	LF.
MERKLE	1B.		STAHL	1B.
HERZOG	3B.		GARDNER	3B.
MEYERS	C.		WAGNER	SS.
FLETCHER	SS.		CARRIGAN	C.
MATHEWSON	P.		WOOD	P.

During the coming series for the world's baseball championship between the New York Giants of the National League and the Boston Red Sox of the American League the New York Times will bulletin every ball pitched, every putout, every base hit, every run scored and in fact every play of the games on a large electric scoreboard, erected on the north side of the Times Building. The board, which is sixteen feet in length and seven feet high will contain the batting orders of the two clubs, show what player is at bat and the result of every ball pitched will be flashed on the board, showing whether the ball was hit safely or fouled, whether it was a ball or strike, whether it resulted in a putout or an error.

While the series is in progress, in both New York and Boston, a special wire will be run direct from the playing field to the New York Times. An operator at the Times Building will immediately flash the information on the electric scoreboard, so the fans will know the result of every pitched ball almost as soon as the ball is hit or reaches the catcher's hands. Separate tables on the large board show the number of balls or strikes for each batsman, as well as the number of outs already made in the inning. Other lights will show the runners on bases and these lights will continue along the base lines and cross the plate when a run is scored. Every time a runner gets on base the light will show his progress around the paths.

All games are scheduled to begin at 2 o'clock and the New York Times electric scoreboard will get into action as soon as the first ball is pitched, showing every detail of the game until the final putout in the last inning.

Figure 3-32B   *(New York Times)*

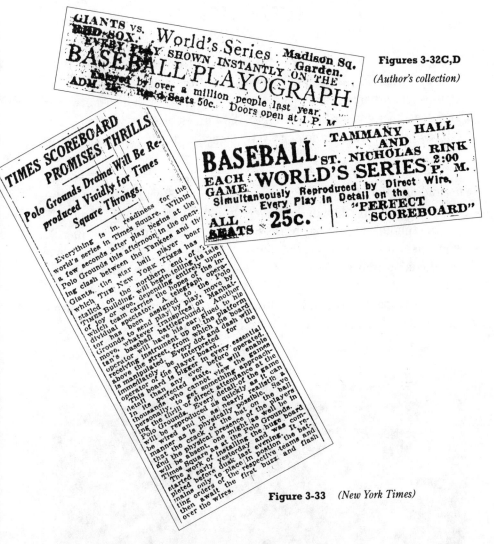

Figures 3-32C,D

(Author's collection)

Figure 3-33   *(New York Times)*

▲ *Figure 3-33* The 1921 World Series, the first for the New York Yankees. The crowd was estimated at 15,000, and some people had to use binoculars to see the board.

The heyday of telegraphic baseball would end with that World Series. *The New York Times* reported: "Jamming every inch of space not strenuously preserved by the police, the gathering impeded pedestrian and vehicular traffic to such an extent that it has been deemed best to discontinue the operation of the board. *The Times,* therefore, will post no more bulletins of the championship games."

But there was another reason for the demise of telegraphic baseball. The 1921 World Series was the first to be broadcast over *radio*.

RADIO DAYS

▼ *Figure 3-34* Regularly scheduled radio broadcasts began in 1920. The following July, the first sporting event on radio was heard—the Dempsey/Carpentier fight. On August 5, 1921, a baseball game was broadcast by radio for the first time. The Pirates beat the Phillies 8–5 at Forbes Field. Phillie outfielder Cy Williams hit the first radio homer in the fourth inning.

The game was broadcast over KDKA in Pittsburgh, the first operating radio station. Only three million American homes had a radio at the time, and only a fraction of those were tuned in to the historic game.

The announcer that day was 26-year-old Harold Arlin (seen here), who was a foreman at Westinghouse. Arlin sat in a box behind home plate, talking into a telephone that had been converted into a microphone.

"I was just a nobody, and our broadcast—back then, at least—wasn't that big a deal," Arlin said years later. He died in 1986 at age 90.

Figure 3-34   *(National Baseball Library, Cooperstown, NY)*

It was clear that baseball was onto something good. *Imagining* the game from its sounds was a good substitute for being there, and sometimes it was better. Millions of people who had never attended a baseball game were exposed to the sport, and many became fans. Even today, many fans like to watch games on TV with the sound off while listening to the play-by-play over radio. "Baseball's theatre of the mind," Curt Smith called it in his history of broadcasting, *Voices of the Game.*

Stores that sold radios set up speakers outside, and people would gather to listen. Cars would pull over to listen. There were no transistor radios or car radios.

By the early 1930s, there were 18 million radios in America. By 1936, 13 of the 16 teams regularly broadcast their games (only the New York teams banned radio, and they came around in 1939). By 1949 there were 39 million radios in the country, and two-thirds of them tuned in to hear the Yankees and Dodgers go at it in the World Series that year.

▲ The first athlete-broadcaster was Jack Graney, the voice of the Indians, in 1932. Graney was an outfielder for Cleveland from 1908 to 1922, hitting .250 with 18 home runs. He led the league in walks twice.

▲ **Radio Re-creations.**   Radio stations didn't send announcers on the road in the 1920s. Instead, they would *simulate* games in a studio using information telephoned or telegraphed from the ball park. Two months after Harold Arlin went on the air, Tommy Cowan, in a studio in Newark, performed the first radio re-creation of a baseball game. It was Game 1 of the 1921 World Series between the New York Yankees and New York Giants. If live radio was the next best thing to being at the ballpark, a re-creation was the next best thing to live radio.

Here's how it worked: There would be a telegraph operator in the press box, and another at the hometown radio station. The press box man would watch the action on the field and turn it into shorthand dots and dashes. "B1H," for example, meant ball one, high." "S1L" indicated "strike one, low."

A studio announcer would receive these snippets of information and announce the game as if he were actually watching it. Arch McDonald was known as the "Rembrandt of the Re-Creation" and would sometimes do them from the window of a drugstore in Washington.

To enhance the theater of the mind, sound effects would fill the background—vendors hawking hot dogs, umpires barking *"Yerrrrr Outtt!,"* infield chatter, bench jockeying. Whacking a stick against a hollow block of wood made a dandy *crack* of the bat. A canned soundtrack of fans cheering was adjusted softer or louder depending on what was happening.

After World War II, baseball had become so popular that radio stations sent their announcers on road trips to follow their team. It was no longer necessary to do re-creations back at the studio. By the early 1950s, re-creations were history. By 1955, virtually every major league baseball game was broadcast live.

One re-creationist went on to bigger and better things. Ronald Reagan (next page) re-created Cubs and White Sox games in the 1930s for WHO in Des Moines, Iowa.

Reagan enjoyed telling the story of the time he was doing a Cubs-Cardinals game when the telegraph wire suddenly went dead. Dizzy Dean was on the mound at the time, and Billy Jurges had just stepped up to the plate. Reagan was sitting in the studio with thousands of fans hanging on every word, but nothing was coming out of the teletype.

Reagan was forced to improvise, hoping he could stall until the technical problem was cleared up. He told the listeners that Dean picked up the resin bag and shook off a couple of signs. Then Reagan had Jurges hit a foul ball behind third base. He had two imaginary kids fighting over the ball. He had Jurges foul off another one that just missed being a home run.

"About six minutes and forty-five seconds later I think I had set a world record for someone standing at the plate," Reagan recalled later.

When the wire finally came back on, the future president of the United States was informed that Jurges had popped out on the first pitch.

▲ **Rhubarbs and Radios.**   There are many theories about why a baseball argument is called a "rhubarb." One of the most interesting is that in the early days of radio, when the director wanted the sound of an angry mob, he would gather a few actors around the microphone and have them murmur, *"Rhubarb . . . rhubarb . . . rhubarb."*

▲ The term "radio ball" is used by players to describe a pitch that is so fast, you can only *hear* it.

Figure 3-35   *(AP/Wide World Photos)*

TELEVISION

▶ *Figure 3-36*   Radio with pictures—what a concept! The first televised baseball game, the first televised sporting event, in fact, was broadcast by NBC on May 17, 1939. It was a college game between Columbia and

Figure 3-36 *(New York Times)*

GAMES ARE TELEVISED

Major League Baseball Makes Its Radio Camera Debut

Major league baseball made its television debut here yesterday as the Dodgers and Reds battled through two games at Ebbets Field before two prying electrical "eyes" of station W2XBS in the Empire State Building. One "eye" or camera was placed near the visiting players' dugout, or behind the right-hand batters' position. The other was in a second-tier box back of the catcher's box and commanded an extensive view of the field when outfield plays were made.

Over the video-sound channels of the station, television-set owners as far away as fifty miles viewed the action and heard the roar of the crowd, according to the National Broadcasting Company.

It was not the first time baseball was televised by the NBC. Last May at Baker Field a game between Columbia and Princeton was caught by the cameras. However, to those who, over the television receivers, saw last May's contest as well as those yesterday, it was apparent that considerable progress has been made in the technical requirements and apparatus for this sort of outdoor pick-up, where the action is fast. At times it was possible to catch a fleeting glimpse of the ball as it sped from the pitcher's hand toward home plate.

Princeton at Baker Field. The camera was positioned in the stands behind home plate.

"We pleaded with the umps to be more emphatic with their calls," recalled announcer Bill Stern. "We actually prayed that all the batters would strike out because that was the one thing that the camera could record." Princeton won 2–1 in 10 innings.

Three months after the Columbia-Princeton game, on August 26, the first major league game was televised—a doubleheader between the Brooklyn Dodgers and Cincinnati Reds at Ebbets Field. A second camera near the visitors' dugout was added to give a different slant on the action.

The game wasn't much to look at, but it was real, live moving pictures of a baseball game. A TV critic with *The New York Times* marveled, "At times it was possible to catch a fleeting glimpse of the ball as it sped from the pitcher's hand toward home plate." The Reds won the first game 5–2, and the Dodgers took the nightcap 6–1. There were only 100 to 200 TV sets in New York at the time.

▼ *Figure 3-37*   The announcer of that first televised major league game was Red Barber (seen here), who sat right in the stands. In addition to calling the game, Barber had the honor of introducing the baseball world to televised *commercials.*

"First I put on a service station cap and talked about Mobil Oil," recalled Barber. "Then I held up a bar of soap that was 99 and 44/100th percent pure. But the big extravaganza was for Wheaties. I poured out an individual serving, added bananas, sugar and cream and said: 'Folks, this is the Breakfast of Champions.'"

Figure 3-37   *(National Baseball Library, Cooperstown, NY)*

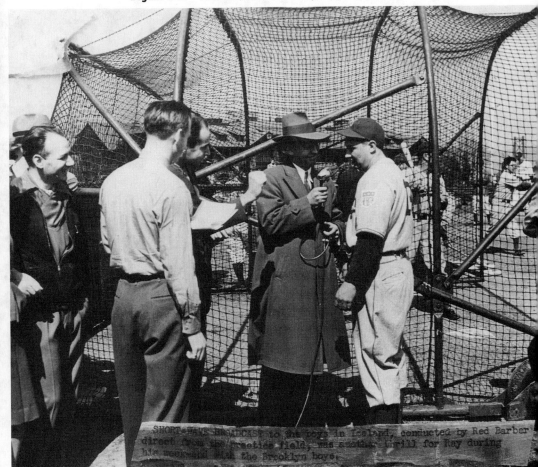

SHORT-WAVE BROADCAST to the boys in Iceland, conducted by Red Barber direct from the practice field, was another thrill for Ray during his weekend with the Brooklyn boys.

▼ *Figures 3-38A, B*   America waited for the boys to return from World War II to fall in love with television. The World Series was televised for the first time in 1947, and that seven-game struggle between the Yankees and Dodgers is still considered one of the best ever. As the ad shows, that Series was used as a marketing device to sell television sets.

TV manufacturers placed sets in public areas to attract potential buyers. This photo was taken in Boston Common during Game 1 of the 1948 World Series between the Cleveland Indians and the Boston Braves.

CBS broadcast the first baseball game in color in 1951, and the same year the World Series was watched coast to coast for the first time. The center-field camera shot was introduced during the 1957 World Series. The first live game broadcast overseas took place on July 23, 1962, between the Cubs and Phillies.

Figure 3-38A   *(AP/Wide World Photos)*

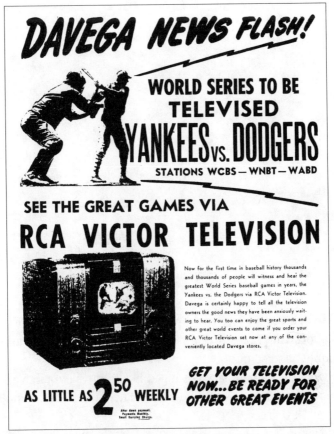

Figure 3-38B   *(Author's collection)*

TOYS AND GAMES

One of the earliest baseball-related patents, granted in 1868, was for a baseball *simulation.* Inventor Francis Sebring was a pitcher for the Empire Base Ball Club of New York. Sebring lived in Hoboken, New Jersey, a hotbed of baseball in the nineteenth century. Alexander Cartwright and his Knickerbockers had played what is believed to be the first organized game of baseball there 23 years earlier.

Sebring was on a ferry from Hoboken to Manhattan to visit an injured teammate when he came up with the idea for "Parlor Base-Ball." It was sort of a primitive pinball game. A spring at the pitcher's box propelled a penny (about the size of today's quarter) toward home plate. A little bat

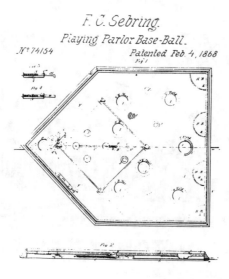

F. C. Sebring.
Playing Parlor Base-Ball.
Nº 74154   Patented Feb. 4, 1868

Figure 3-39   *(U.S. Patent Office)*

attached to another spring would whip around and hit the coin, sending it into one of many holes in the board, which were labeled "out," "single," "double," and so on.

Notice that the game board is shaped like home plate (above). This is an amazing coincidence—the five-sided plate would not be adopted by baseball for 32 years.

No copies of "Parlor Base-Ball" are known to exist, and it may have never gone into production. There have been dozens of other mechanical baseball games with little bats striking balls and little figures moving around a little diamond, including a direct copy of Sebring's game by Chief Zimmer, a major league catcher from 1884 to 1903.

▶ *Figures 3-40A, B, C* A number of games have been developed that test baseball skills and are commonly seen at country fairs and amusement parks. Edward Harberson's 1915 "Base Ball Machine" had a built-in pitching gun for batting practice. Herbert Shaules' 1906 "Target" tested the player's throwing accuracy. So did David Elseroad's clearly named "Baseball Game Apparatus Including Movable Target Panels at Which a Baseball Is Thrown by the Player." This 1964 invention had two targets, a strike zone and a first baseman. When either target was hit with the ball, a light would turn on. Several other amusement-type baseball games are seen in Chapter 2 under "Ball Returners."

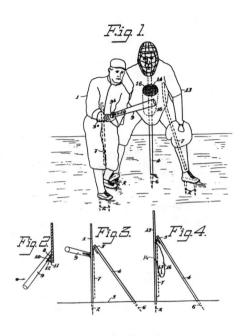

May 19, 1964   D. C. ELSEROAD   3,133,733
BASEBALL GAME APPARATUS INCLUDING MOVABLE TARGET PANELS
AT WHICH A BASEBALL IS THROWN BY THE PLAYER
Filed March 15, 1963

No. 811,963.

PATENTED FEB. 6, 1906.

H. A. SHAULES.
TARGET.
APPLICATION FILED JULY 3, 1905.

Figure 3-40A   *(U.S. Patent Office)*

Figure 3-40B   *(U.S. Patent Office)*

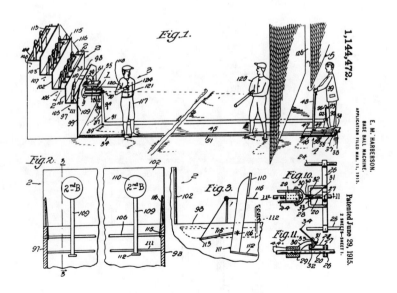

Figure 3-40C   *(U.S. Patent Office)*

▼ **Statistical Games.** *Figure 3-41* The first statistical game was "National Pastime," which was patented in 1925 by Clifford A. Van Beek, of Green Bay, Wisconsin. The game included dice, play sheets, and stat cards for the players of 1930. Unfortunately, Van Beek's printer went bankrupt during the Depression and the artwork for the game became tied up in legal proceedings.

Van Beek's idea was carried on and refined with "All-Star Baseball," which was invented by Ethan Allen in the late 1940s. Allen was a journeyman outfielder and career .300 hitter from 1926 to 1938. He received a master's degree in education in 1932, while playing for the New York Giants. After his playing days, he coached a young George Bush at Yale.

Allen's innovation was a round card with a spinner on it for each player. The card for sluggers like Babe Ruth had a large part of the circle devoted to home runs, walks, and strikeouts. The card for Richie Ashburn, who was a good hitter with little power, had a large area for singles and doubles.

"It occurred to me that a player's batting record could be graphed on a circle," Allen told *The Wall Street Journal* in 1991. "Once I hit upon

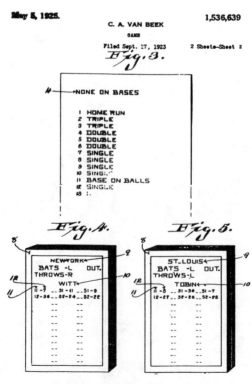

Figure 3-41   *(U.S. Patent Office)*

that, putting the game together wasn't difficult." "All-Star Baseball" was rejected by every large toy company until Allen took it to Chicago-based Cadaco. Their response: "Good idea! We'll make it!"

They still make it today. In Allen's day, players weren't compensated for the use of their records. Now they receive royalties. Babe Ruth's estate alone collects about $2,000 a year from "All-Star Baseball." Ethan Allen passed away in 1993.

The only flaw in the game was that pitchers didn't matter. That problem was taken care of by the next generation of card-based baseball simulations, "APBA" (1951) and "Strat-O-Matic Baseball" (1963). Both of these hugely successful games work like this: The "manager" selects a lineup, rolls the dice, and reads directions corresponding to the numbers on a series of charts ("APBA") or on player cards ("Strat-O-Matic"). The charts and cards take into account the player's strengths and weaknesses in various situations. APBA (pronounced ap-bah) stands for American Professional Baseball Association.

▼ **Computer Games.** *Figure 3-42* When the personal computer came on the scene in the 1980s, baseball software simulations quickly followed. Instead of dice, spinners, cards and other paraphernalia, all vital information was stored and tabulated by the computer. Players

Figure 3-42 *(Electronic Arts)*

could pick lineups from real or imaginary players, set the defense, make pitching changes, pinch-hit, steal, or just sit back with a beer and watch the computer punch out an entire game in five minutes. Want to see the 1927 Yankees play the 1969 Mets? No problem.

One of the most popular games—a marvel of baseball intricacy—has been "Earl Weaver Baseball," published by Electronic Arts and created by Eddie Dombrower and Weaver himself (seen here). The latest version of the game includes all the current major league players. Each position player has over 50 hitter/fielder ratings (power, running, range, and so forth), and pitchers are rated 30 ways (lefty versus righty stats, durability, salary, ground ball/fly out ratio).

The screen can be configured for a modern ballpark or a classic field like the Polo Grounds, or you can build your own stadium dimensions. The game boasts "perfect baseball physics," with camera views that look like televised baseball. When the batter steps up to the plate, you see a view from behind. If he bangs a shot to third, you switch to a view from the first-base side. If your third baseman made a great play, you can watch an instant replay, in slow-mo and freeze frame. Digitized baseball sounds—the crack of the bat, the umpire—add to the realism.

Players can compete against Earl Weaver, Walter Alston, Joe McCarthy, or dozens of famous and not-so-famous managers (based on their actual tendencies), or construct a manager by answering questions posed by the computer ("If your starter has thrown 100 pitches and you're ahead by three runs, when would you go to the bullpen?"). You can even create your own league—draft players, hire free agents, generate a schedule, and play ball.

▶ *Figure 3-43* Manager extraordinaire Tony La Russa (next page) lent his expertise to "Tony La Russa's Ultimate Baseball," which is published by Strategic Simulations of Sunnyvale, California. "La Russa" features the digitized voice of sports announcer Ron Barr shouting, "Chin music!" "Chalk up a K!" and other baseballisms. The game was created by Don Daglow, who was part of the team that created "Earl Weaver Baseball."

Orel Hershiser, Reggie Jackson, Bo Jackson, Pete Rose, and other stars have lent their names to computer baseball simulations.

▶ *Figures 3-44A, B* Two freeze frames of "Tony La Russa's Ultimate Baseball."

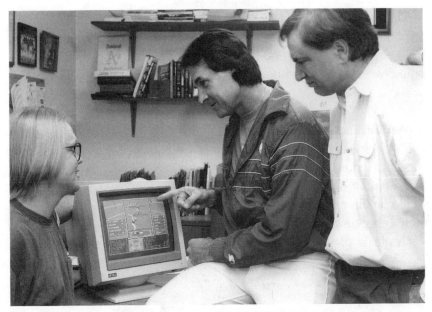

Figure 3-43 *(Strategic Simulations, Inc.)*

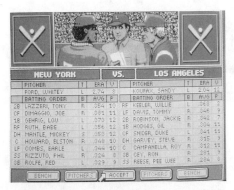

Figure 3-44A *(Strategic Simulations, Inc.)*

Figure 3-44B *(Strategic Simulations, Inc.)*

▲ **Rotisserie.** One night in 1980, a group of baseball nuts got to-gether for dinner in a New York restaurant and cooked up a new form of baseball. The name of the restaurant was *La Rotisserie Francaise.*

Rotisserie baseball—frequently called "fantasy baseball"—uses the actual statistics of active players during the current season. When base-ball season begins, each team "manager" selects 14 batters and nine pitchers. After every game, points are awarded based on performance. The "team" with the most points at the end of the season wins the pen-nant (sometimes a bottle of Yoo-Hoo poured over the manager's head).

The enormous popularity of this game has spawned an entire industry of hopelessly addicted players, computer statistic services, software, tip sheets, and newsletters. It's no wonder baseball attendance and TV ratings are down—everybody's home playing *simulations* of baseball.

▼ **Mechanical Baseball Bank.** *Figures 3-45A, B* James H. Bowen of Philadelphia patented this ingenious mechanical bank in 1888. A coin was inserted under the pitcher's thumb. When his arm was pulled back and a button on the right side of the catcher was pressed, the pitcher would fire an underhand fastball into the catcher's belly while the batter took a check swing.

Originals of this bank sell for $1,500 or more on the "racist col-

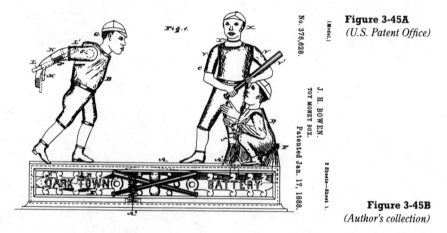

Figure 3-45A
(U.S. Patent Office)

Figure 3-45B
(Author's collection)

lectible" market. Notice that the name on the patent, "DARK TOWN BATTERY," was changed to "HOME TOWN BATTERY" on the version in the photo. Also, the players in the patent look vaguely black, and those in the photo are definitely white.

The bank was patented the same year baseball's color barrier went up. It was in 1887 that Chicago White Stockings manager Cap Anson refused to allow his players to take the field if opposing teams had black players on them. Anson's popularity kept all blacks out of the majors, and the doors remained shut for 60 years.

▼ **The Personal Computer.**   *Figure 3-46*   The PC touched us all in the 1980s, and there was a widespread assumption that anything involving numbers would become "computerized." Naturally, baseball, with its emphasis on statistics, would fall under the computer's spell. Dozens of newspaper and magazine articles appeared on the subject, invariably titled "PCs Break into the Lineup," "The Microchipped Diamond," and so on.

The computer *has* had an effect on baseball. Computer-literate managers accurately track player performance and use the information to write lineups, position fielders, and determine how to pitch to troublesome batters. Broadcasters pull up relevant stats before a play is finished. Reporters zip their stories to their newspapers by modem. Player agents negotiate salaries with an armful of printouts showing that their clients had a great season, and management arrives with an equally

Figure 3-46   *(Electronic Arts)*

thick printout proving the opposite. Scouts carry laptops into the hinter-lands, hoping they'll discover the next DiMaggio.

But having a computer at your side, on your lap, or even in the dugout is no guarantee of success. Before he was hired by the New York Mets, American League Manager of the Year Jeff Torborg had the Mets purchase a $50,000 computer program to assist him in his job. Torborg was fired 37 games into the 1993 season, when the last-place Mets had already fallen 15 games out. They finished with the worst record in baseball.

"All of the fascination and the speculation about the computer, about 'what it is going to do' and 'how it will change things' in baseball and in other areas is completely misguided," claims Bill James, "because it is not going to do anything and it is not going to change anything."

▶ **The Baseball Computer.**   *Figure 3-47*   Who was the fattest guy to ever play in the majors?

This it the question I was burning to ask Franklin's "Big League Baseball Encyclopedia," a five-ounce computer. The little thing stores 620,000 batting statistics and 270,000 pitching statistics—data on any-one who ever played in the big leagues. It's like having every baseball card ever printed in your shirt pocket.

I punched in MAX WT, and 17 seconds later I had my answer—Wal-ter "Jumbo" Brown, a 295-pound behemoth who pitched for five teams from 1925 to 1941. Jumbo won 33 games, lost 31, and saved 29 over his undistinguished career.

As an encyclopedia, the computer can't hold the jock of *The Baseball Encyclopedia*. It doesn't include fielding averages, league leaders, place of birth, place of death, pinch-hitting stats, or postseason stats. The tiny screen displays only two years at a time. So if you want to compare what Babe Ruth hit as a rookie in 1914 (.200) with his final season in 1935 (.181), you have to tap a key 20 times. With the book, of course, you just glance two inches down the page.

The real strength of "Big League Baseball" is its ability to compile lists in seconds that would take weeks with a book. Say you want to find out which players hit the most career triples. You simply punch MAX 3B. In 13 seconds you have your list: Sam Crawford, Ty Cobb, Honus Wagner, Tris Speaker, Jake Beckley, and so on.

You can take it further by adding "limiters" and "qualifiers." A truly obsessed fan could instruct the computer, "Name all the left-handed

Figure 3-47   *(Franklin Electronic Publishers, Inc.)*

American League pitchers with the lowest ERAs who pitched more than 1,000 innings between 1940 and 1949." Or, "Give me the highest triples to at-bats ratio by an American League hitter in the 1930s with 100 or more at bats."

I go for the offbeat stats, myself. If you type MAX AGE, you get the oldest men to play the game: Satchel Paige (58), Minnie Minoso (57), Nick Altrock (56), Jim O'Rourke (53), Charley O'Leary (51), and so forth. Type MIN AGE and you get the youngest: John Greening (15), Joe Nuxhall (15), and a bunch of 16-year-olds—Leonidas Lee, Milt Scott, Piggy Ward, Tom Hess, Joe Stanley, Coonie Blank, Jim Curry, and Rogers McKee.

Or how about the lightest guys in the majors? First, of course is Eddie Gaedel, the 65-pound midget who came to bat once for the St. Louis Browns in 1951. He's followed by curveball inventor Candy Cummings (120), Larry Corcoran (120), Dummy Leitner (120), Yale Murphy (125), George Paynter (125), and Hall of Famer Johnny Evers (125).

A search of the nickname "Red" turns up 94 players. The tallest members of the Hall of Fame are Eppa Rixey, Don Drysdale, and Ferguson Jenkins, all of whom were six foot five. The shortest was Wee Willie Keeler, at five foot four.

In searching for the worst earned run average in history, I learned that there have been 19 players whose ERA is listed as "infinite." The highest recorded ERA is 162.00 by Andy Sommerville, whose entire career consisted of a third of an inning for Brooklyn in 1894. In that outing he gave up five walks, one hit, and six runs. Poor slob took the loss, too.

My special fondness, however, is fat guys. The fattest Hall of Famer is

Reds catcher Ernie Lombardi, whose 230 pounds dwarfed even Babe Ruth (215). Garland Buckeye is the fattest left-hander, and also the fattest switch-hitter. The fattest guy with more than 400 home runs is Dave Winfield. The fattest guy to steal more than 100 bases is Dave Parker. When it comes to the fattest guys with 1,000 or more at bats, 255-pound Frank Howard takes the cake, so to speak.

▲ The Future of Baseball Simulation.   The television will merge with the computer and give birth to truly interactive baseball. We will be able to watch a game on TV and select our own camera angles via remote control. We will be able to instantly calculate the odds of various managerial decisions, predict what the real manager will do, and compete against millions of armchair second-guessers sitting in their homes. We will be able to don virtual reality helmets and fulfill every fan's true fantasy—to get a shot at playing in the majors.

BALLPARK CUISINE

▶ Buy Me Some Peanuts and . . .   *Figures 3-48A, B, C*   Cracker Jack was invented in 1893 by a Chicago man named F.W. Rueckheim. He had arrived from Germany in 1871 and used his $200 life savings to open a popcorn stand. At the Chicago Columbian Exposition in 1893, F.W. and his brother Louis introduced a combination of popcorn, peanuts, and molasses. It was a big hit, and quickly became a staple at ballparks.

The snack got its name in 1896 when a salesman munching on it for the first time exclaimed, "That's a cracker jack!" Somewhere along the line "crackerjack" came to mean a good player, or a person who is good in any particular field. A customer thought up the slogan, "The more you eat, the more you want."

Cracker Jack got a big boost in 1908 when it was mentioned in the popular song "Take Me Out to the Ballgame." The logo with Sailor Jack and his dog Bingo appeared during World War I. Sailor Jack was modeled after F.W.'s grandson Robert, who died of pneumonia soon after the character appeared on the box.

Starting in 1921, Cracker Jack munchers were likely to find a tiny magnifying glass, book, tattoo, or some other prize in every box. The

Figure 3-48A   *(Borden)*

Figure 3-48B   *(Borden)*

Figure 3-48C   *(Borden)*

toys have become collectibles, and some are worth hundreds of dollars.

F.W.'s company was purchased by Borden, Inc., in 1964. They pop 18 to 20 tons of corn a day to keep up with the continuing demand for Cracker Jack. That's the largest use of popcorn in the world.

▶ **They Always Taste Better at the Ballpark.**   *Figure 3-49*   There are several theories about who invented the hot dog. One says a pie vendor named Charles Feltman came up with the idea in 1867 as a way to compete with pie vendors on Coney Island. Another says an Englishman named Harry Stevens sold the first hot dog during a baseball game at the Polo Grounds in 1901.

We know more about Stevens than Feltman, and besides, this is a baseball book, so let's go with the Stevens theory.

Harry Mozley Stevens (next page) arrived from Derby, England, in 1882 with his wife and three kids. The family settled in Ohio and Harry got a job working in a steel mill. One day he attended a ballgame in Columbus. He purchased a scorecard for five cents, but felt it was almost worthless for identifying the players on the field. Stevens persuaded the owner of the team to allow *him* to print a better scorecard.

He did, and went through the stands wearing a red coat and straw hat, shouting, "You can't tell the players without a scorecard!" Fans bought "Scorecard Harry's" new scorecards, and Stevens was awarded a five-year contract to provide them for the Columbus ballpark.

Seeing an opportunity, Stevens went to other ballparks and did the same thing. Soon he was selling peanuts, beer, soda, and ice cream, too, and by the 1890s he was running the concessions at most parks. Legend has it that Harry played a role in the popularity of the drinking straw— he offered them along with sodas so fans wouldn't miss a second of action while they were swigging.

Anyway, back to the hot dog. It was a chilly summer day in 1901 and Harry wasn't selling much ice cream. The Polo Grounds was in a German neighborhood, so he sent out for small wursts, German frankfurter sausages known as "dachshunds." He boiled them and slipped them inside rolls—so fans would be able to hold them without burning their hands, getting messy, or needing plates or utensils.

Harry and his vendors took the taste treat around the stands yelling, "Get your red hots!" Newspaper cartoonist Tad Dorgan dubbed the new sandwich the "hot dog."

The phrase "hot dog" came to mean a player who puts on a performance for the sake of fans. It has been suggested that these play-

Figure 3-49 *(Harry M. Stevens)*

ers are called hot dogs because they play the game *"with relish."*

Harry M. Stevens, who Babe Ruth called "my second dad," died in 1934. But his sons carried on and grandson Joe Stevens is chairman of Harry M. Stevens, Inc., today. Nearly a century after he sold his first hot dog, "Harry M. Stevens" is still a familiar name at ballparks across America.

▼ **Beer and Coke.** *Figure 3-50* An essential piece of baseball equipment in the 1880s was the "German Disturber"—a keg of beer and a dipper positioned in foul territory near third base. When a player reached third safely, he was allowed to take a dipperful of beer.

Figure 3-50

REEVE'S ERYTHROXYLON COCO TROCHE.—Invaluable to Base Ball Players, Cricketers, Rowers, Gymnasts, Athletes, and Sportsmen in general. These Troches are prepared with the pure Extract of the Erythroxylon Coco Leaves. "as used by Weston the American Pedestrian," Cavill, the champion swimmer, and others; carefully selected from Bolivia, which has the reputation of producing the best. Combined with the Extract of Coco is a small proportion of phosphate of lime and other ingredients, which are well-known to have great tonic and invigorating powers. The Troches are convenient and exceedingly pleasant to take, and are now acknowledged throughout the world to be the greatest tonic extant. The proprietor (T. L. Reeve) is now having a pamphlet published containing many testimonials and interesting details from athletes and eminent men, including Sir Robert Christison, M.D., Edinburgh, who has had experience with the Coco and obtained marvelous results. The Pamphlet, when complete, will be forwarded to any address on application. The Troches may be given to delicate children with great advantage. Dose, according to age.
Price, per box, by mail, 25 cents.

Back in the dugout, he might indulge in some coke. That's coke with a small *c*. This 1886 ad boasted of the "great tonic and invigorating powers" of Bolivian cocaine, which "may be given to delicate children with great advantage."

▼ **For the Fan Who Has Everything.**   *Figures 3-51A, B*   An auctioneer in Binghamton, New York, came across this 1940s chair a few years ago. It was purchased sight unseen by American Primitive Gallery in New York City and displayed in a show of baseball folk art. For more comfort, you may prefer Joe Sofa, which can be found at Palazzetti in Philadelphia, New York, Chicago, Dallas, and Toronto.

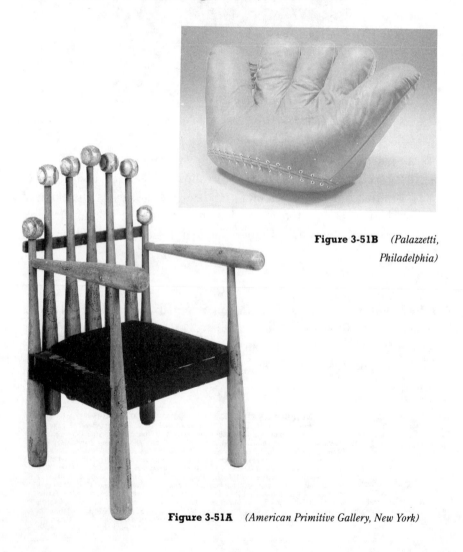

Figure 3-51B   *(Palazzetti, Philadelphia)*

Figure 3-51A   *(American Primitive Gallery, New York)*

4

Baseballs

The First Baseball?   A battered old ball was found in an old trunk in Fly Creek, New York, two miles from Cooperstown. The trunk belonged to a man named Abner Graves, who passed away in 1926 at the age of 92. It was Graves who claimed his boyhood pal Abner Doubleday invented baseball in 1839, sketching the first diamond with a stick in the dirt behind a Cooperstown tailor shop.

Cooperstown resident Stephen C. Clark bought the ball for $5 in 1935 and put it on display in the Cooperstown Village Club with some other early baseball artifacts.

If you build it, they will come . . .

In 1935, National League president Ford Frick realized that if Doubleday had invented baseball in 1839, that meant the game's 100th birthday was four years away. Frick suggested commemorating the centennial with a permanent baseball museum in Cooperstown. The National Baseball Hall of Fame was built.

The theory that Abner Doubleday invented baseball has been totally discredited since then, but nearly half a million fans make the pilgrimage to Cooperstown each year anyway.

Two years before he died, Abner Graves murdered his wife. A jury found him mentally unbalanced. He died in a Pueblo, Colorado, institution for the criminally insane. His ball is still in the Hall of Fame, labeled "the Abner Doubleday Baseball."

▲ **Horses and Cows.**   According to the Hall of Fame, the baseball *cover* was invented by a boy named Ellis Drake. He was in school and drew a picture of his brainstorm while the teacher wasn't looking. Drake never patented the baseball cover, and he never made a dime from his creation.

Horsehide was the standard covering throughout baseball's first century. A shortage of quality horsehide forced a switch to cowhide in 1974. On April 14 of that year in Cincinnati, the first ball with a cowhide cover was used in a major league game.

▶ **The Walnut Ball.**   *Figure 4-1*   At first, baseballs were wound by hand. The inside of the ball was made of twine, chamois, or sheepskin. A young Georgia boy named Tyrus Cobb recalled that he would wind yarn around a rubber ball and have a leathermaker sew a cover on it. In return, Cobb would run a few errands for the leathermaker. Dizzy Dean once said the first ball he owned was a walnut with string wound around it. It was held together by a cover made of shoe tongues.

Pioneer pitcher and sporting goods mogul Albert Spalding (next page) wrote: "It was usually made on the spot by some boy offering up his woolen socks as an oblation, and these were raveled and wound round a bullet, a handful of strips cut from a rubber overshoe, a piece of cork or almost anything. The winding of this ball was an art, and whoever could excel in this art was looked upon as a superior being."

Balls ranged from five to six ounces, from 8.5 to 11 inches in circumference. A good-fielding team would make loose, soft baseballs. A team of sluggers would wind tight, hard, lively balls. Even the *best* handmade balls were hard to hit very far. Home runs were rare, and "scientific" hitting, running, and fielding were the order of the day.

As baseball spread across the country, it became necessary to have more baseballs, and balls that were uniform in size and liveliness. The first manufacturers of baseballs, in the 1850s, were John Van Horn of New York and Harvey Rose of Brooklyn. They made three-ounce balls with a core of cut-up, melted old rubber shoes wrapped with a cover of sheepskin. The weight and size of the official baseball changed dramatically over the next few decades, but the size of ball hasn't changed since 1876, and the inside has remained virtually the same since 1910.

Figure 4-1   *(Spalding)*

▼ **The First Patent for a Baseball.**   *Figure 4-2*   John Giblin's 1875 innovation was a "heart" of palm leaves surrounded by woolen yarn, cotton thread, and a rubber cover. Giblin, a Boston man, didn't claim that his was the *first* baseball. He called his invention an "improvement in base-balls" and wrote, "It will outlast very many of the leather-covered balls, and, having no seams or sewing as they have, is not so liable to injure the hands of a player."

Figure 4-2   *(U.S. Patent Office)*

▸ **The Ding-Dong Ball.** *Figure 4-3* Six months after John Giblin was awarded his patent, another Boston man, Samuel Hipkiss, patented a baseball with a *bell* inside it. As with the "ding-dong base" described in Chapter 3, the purpose of the bell was to assist the umpire in making decisions.

Hipkiss wrote: "In the game of 'base' it is occasionally very difficult, if not impossible, to ascertain whether the ball is struck by the bat, the blow being so light, or so aslant on the ball, as to cause the noise of it not to be loud enough to be sufficiently audible; but with the bell within the ball a sound is emitted whenever a ball is struck or caught by a player, the advantage of which will be appreciated by those who understand the games of cricket or base."

John Giblin and Samuel Hipkiss probably knew each other. Notice that they used the same attorney and witness on their patent applications.

▸ **The Baseball Makers.** *Figures 4-4A, B* Most of the important innovations in baseballs over the next 40 years would come from Alfred J. Reach (see woodcut illustration) and Benjamin Shibe (right in photo, holding cane). Reach was born in London in 1840. He came to the United States as an infant and was raised in Brooklyn. The five-six left-hander became the star second baseman of the Philadelphia Athletics in 1863, and is often referred to as the first baseball player to openly receive money for his services. By 1874 Reach was managing the team, and the same year he opened a store in Philadelphia selling baseball equipment. Almost immediately, he retired as a player.

Benjamin Franklin Shibe was born in Philadelphia in 1833. "Uncle Ben" and his brother John opened a hardware store there, manufacturing baseballs on the side. Eventually, the baseballs took over the business.

Al Reach wanted to get into the manufacturing end of things, and in 1881 A. J. Reach Company and J. D. Shibe & Company teamed up (though they maintained separate offices). Shibe was the expert mechanic, Reach the salesman.

▸ **The Seamless Baseball, 1883.** *Figures 4-5A,B,C* Shibe and Reach's first innovation was a baseball without seams. Early baseballs tended to come apart at the seams, so naturally it was determined that a

S. HIPKISS.
BASE-BALL.

No. 172,315. Patented Jan. 18, 1876.

Figure 4-3 *(U.S. Patent Office)*

Figures 4-4A,B *(National Baseball Library, Cooperstown, NY)*

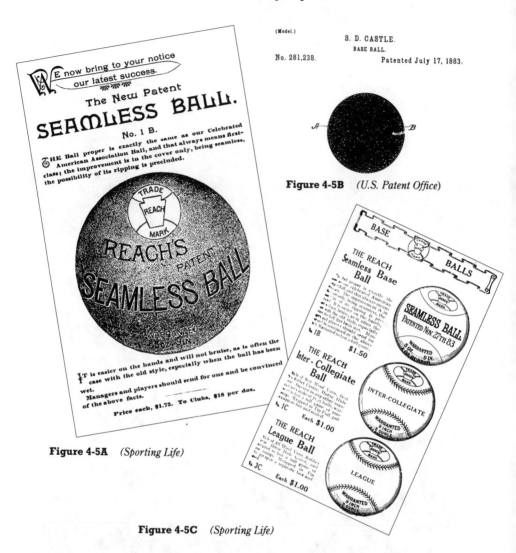

Figure 4-5A *(Sporting Life)*

Figure 4-5B *(U.S. Patent Office)*

Figure 4-5C *(Sporting Life)*

seamless ball was desirable. This "improvement" was patented by Samuel D. Castle of Bridgeport, Connecticut, and marketed by A. J. Reach Company.

"My invention consists in the process of covering balls by dipping them in a liquid solution of gutta-percha, dissolved in bisulphide of carbon," wrote Castle. He claimed his ball was more durable and less expensive to produce.

However, seamless balls made it nearly impossible to throw a curveball, which had been invented in the 1860s and was sweeping the national pastime. The seamless ball went into baseball's trash heap.

A century later, wind tunnel experiments would reveal that knuckleballs and spitballs are *also* dependent on the baseball's seams. Both pitches are thrown with little or no rotation. The seams bump against the air around the ball, causing it to break one or more times on the way to the plate.

The same year the seamless ball was introduced, Al Reach was approached about starting a National League team in Philadelphia. He became the first president of the Philadelphia Phillies and made baseball pioneer Harry Wright the manager the following year. The Phillies are the oldest continuous, one-name, one-city franchise in the major leagues.

▼ **Double Seams.**   *Figures 4-6A, B, C*   The seamless ball idea abandoned, Reach and Shibe came up with *another* idea to hold their balls together—*double* seams. Daniel M. Shibe, another member of the Shibe family, received the patent for this invention.

"So far as I am aware," wrote Shibe, "the covers of baseballs are sewed by a single line of stitches on the seams or edges of the part of the cover, which single line of stitches proves inadequate to fully serve

Figure 4-6A   *(Sporting Life)*

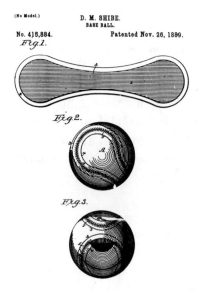

(No Model.)   D. M. SHIBE.
BASE BALL.

No. 4]6,884.   Patented Nov. 26, 1889.

Fig.1.

Fig.2.

Fig.3.

Figure 4-6B   *(U.S. Patent Office)*

Figure 4-6C

TRADE REACH MARK

AmericanAssociation
DOUBLE STITCH
ADOPTED BY THE AMERICAN ASSOCIATION

WARRANTED

THE REACH BALL
When *merit* is the *best*, it stands
pre-eminently alone as

The Best

It keeps its shape
It gives satisfaction
It is guaranteed

MAKERS

A. J. REACH CO.
PHILADELPHIA, PA.

the purpose. The material of the cover tears out or the thread breaks, owing to the rough usage the ball is subjected to." Shibe's solution was to sew reinforced saddler's stitches alongside the usual "catstitches."

In the long run, the real solution was simply better-made baseballs with a single stitch.

▶ **Dead Balls.** *Figures 4-7A, B* In 1886, it was not unsettling to see an ad for a ball that said "BOY'S DEAD" on it. The dead ball wasn't just an *era.* Manufacturers actually *called* their balls dead and even *boasted* about how dead they were.

Notice that Spalding's 1887 Professional Dead is "warranted to last a game of nine innings." Baseballs were not discarded when they got a little smudge on them. Foul balls were not souvenirs; they were expected to be returned by the fans. A baseball would stay in the game even if it was brown, misshapen, and waterlogged.

That being the case, baseball strategy was to get as many runs as possible *early* in the game, because by the later innings the ball would be a

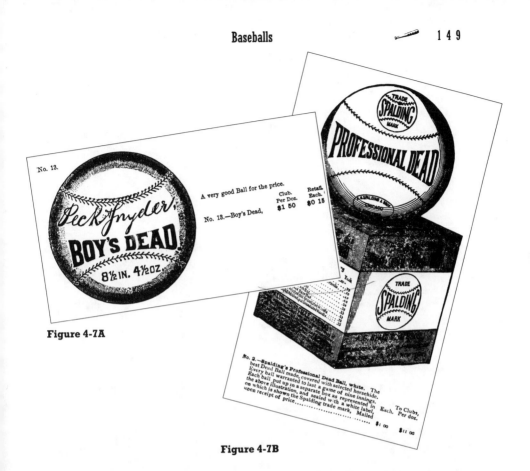

Figure 4-7A

Figure 4-7B

lumpy mess. In the Spalding ad on page 153, New York Giant catcher Roger Bresnahan testified to the fact that with the new 1911 ball, "You can make a home run in the ninth inning just as easily as in the first."

▶ **Making Baseballs.** *Figures 4-8A, B, C* Various inventors created machines to mass produce baseballs. One of the first was patented in 1876 by Wolf Fletcher of Covington, Kentucky. Essentially, it was a hinged wooden block with the mold of two balls carved into it. The baseball maker would fill the molds with balls of twine and other material, close the two halves and pound the two halves together with a mallet.

Thomas P. Taylor of Bridgeport, Connecticut, had another idea. He forced the guts of the ball through a funnel (A), and then compressed them into the shape of a ball with a plunger. The contents were then heated until they became hard.

Both of these machines treated the baseball as if it were a snowball, to be compacted into a sphere. Eventually, inventors learned what little

W. FLECHTER.
MANUFACTURE OF BASE-BALLS.

No. 174,511.

Patented March 7, 1876.

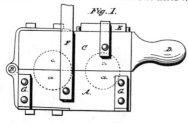

Fig. 1.

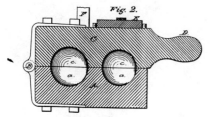

Fig. 2.

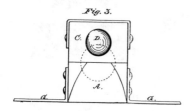

Fig. 3.

Figure 4-8A   *(U.S. Patent Office)*

T. P. TAYLOR.
MANUFACTURE OF BASE BALLS.

No. 277,809.

Patented May 15, 1883.

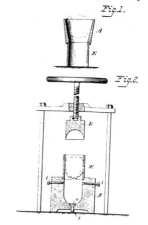

Fig. 1.

Fig. 2.

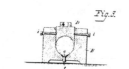

Fig. 3.

Figure 4-8B   *(U.S. Patent Office)*

B. B. NEWELL.
BASE BALL WINDING AND ROLLING MACHINE.

No. 397,303.

Patented Feb. 5, 1889.

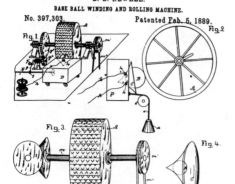

Fig. 1

Fig. 2

Fig. 3.

Fig. 4.

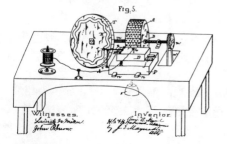

Fig. 5.

Witnesses.

Inventor.

Figure 4-8C   *(U.S. Patent Office)*

boys had known all along—you should take a small spherical object and wind something *around* it until it reaches the proper size. Then, sew a cover over it.

A Boston man named Benjamin Burleigh Newell invented one of the first machines that automated the winding of yarn around a baseball.

"It is well known to be a slow and laborious task to wind a base-ball by hand," Newell wrote in 1889. "In order to make the ball sufficiently solid by such process much pounding is necessary. When the ball has been pounded, the surface of it is softened to such an extent that it becomes necessary to unwind several yards of the yarn and begin anew. Through pounding, unwinding, and winding again much time is consumed, and at best the winding when completed is of variable tension, rendering the ball in this respect defective and unscientific."

Newell's machine kept a consistent tension in the yarn, so unwinding and pounding the baseball into submission became unnecessary.

▼ **The Perfect Ball.** *Figures 4-9A, B* Though he never patented one, Ben Shibe is generally credited with inventing the intricate machines for winding the yarn, cutting covers, and punching holes in the covers to exact specifications. Balls made by Reach and Shibe were wound tightly, and machinery had been perfected to the point that one baseball was virtually identical to another.

By 1883, the A. J. Reach Company assembly line was cranking out a baseball every ten minutes. Trained specialists made balls for the big leagues, and they could turn out 25 a day. A kid could buy a cheap baseball for a nickel, and he could get the best money could buy for 75 cents.

Figures 4-9A,B *(Sporting Life)*

Albert Spalding was expanding *his* sporting goods empire at this time (see page 169), and he bought out Reach and Shibe in 1889. The next year Spalding announced his official league ball was "perfect" and claimed it "cannot be further improved upon."

A. J. Reach & Company continued operating under its own name after it was acquired by Spalding. Reach received $100,000 and an executive position with Spalding, but was free to devote more time to his Phillies.

When the American League was founded in 1901, Reach suggested to Ben Shibe that *he* start a team in Philadelphia too. Shibe formed the Philadelphia Athletics, with a 39-year-old kid named Connie Mack as the manager. Mack would hold that position for the next half-century. Shibe built the first concrete-and-steel ballpark in 1909 and named it after himself.

The new American League used baseballs bearing the Reach trademark, while National League balls said "Spalding" on them. Players swore they could tell the difference between the balls, but it was an open secret that all the balls were made with the same machinery and simply rolled into two baskets.

▶ **The Corked Baseball.** *Figures 4-10A,B* Long after Spalding bought out Al Reach, the Reach name continued to influence baseball. Al's son George Reach (who married Ben Shibe's daughter Mary), became a Spalding executive and received credit for introducing the modern cork-center baseball in 1911.

Up until this time the core of the ball had been made of rubber, with the assumption that the more resilient the core, the more resilient the ball. But in a 1910 patent for a baseball, Ben Shibe wrote that he found the *opposite* to be true.

"I have found that the use of a resilient and yielding core is not essential to produce the resiliency of a base ball of said character, if in fact it does not impair or reduce that quality in the use to which it is subjected by reason of its yielding or absorption of the force of a blow and its tardiness in rebounding from the blow of a bat until after the ball has been driven away."

In other words, rubber is bouncy, but because it doesn't return to its shape until *after* the ball leaves the bat, the bounciness does not translate into liveliness. Instead, Shibe proposed a ball with "rigid, unyielding and inflexible central core."

Cricket players had been using a cork-center ball since 1863, when it

Figure 4-10A

Figure 4-10B   *(New York Times)*

was patented by an Englishman named Weeks. Baseball secretly put new cork-center balls into play during the 1910 World Series. The "lively ball era" had begun.

With the new ball, batting averages, runs, and home runs per game skyrocketed in 1911. Ty Cobb hit .420, his highest average ever and 53 points above his lifetime average. Rookie Shoeless Joe Jackson hit .408, *his* highest average also, and 52 points above his lifetime average.

Pitchers, desperate for an edge, concocted new weapons. Russ Ford of the New York Highlanders came up with the scuffball. Larry Cheney of the Cubs invented the knuckleball after a freak accident—a line drive rammed his thumb into his nose, breaking both of them. Throwing a knuckler the next season, he went 26–10.

Before he died in 1954, George Reach revealed that the 1911 baseball was the liveliest ever.

Every few years, baseball is accused of "juicing up" the ball. In 1920, when Babe Ruth went from an astonishing 29 home runs in a season to an *unbelievable* 59, it was widely believed the ball had been livened. More likely, the hitting revolution of the 1920s was a result of the ban on the spitball and scuffball, and of the effort to get dirty baseballs out of the game.

Rumors of new "rabbit balls" also spread in 1925, 1950, 1956, 1961, 1969, 1977, and 1987. But like the formula for Coca-Cola, whether major league baseball is livening or deadening baseballs remains one of the world's best kept secrets.

Al Reach sold the Phillies in 1902 and retired to Atlantic City. He passed away in 1928 at age 88. Ben Shibe, 89, died in 1922. Baseballs with the brand name "Reach" were sold until 1975, when Spalding finally dropped the name.

▶ *Figure 4-11*   Spalding was the official supplier of major league baseballs for a full century—1876 to 1976. At that time Rawlings took over. The first major league Rawlings baseball was used on April 6, 1977, in Cincinnati. A beanball is occasionally referred to as a "Rawlings lobotomy."

▶ **Inside Baseball.**   *Figures 4-12A, B*   Is it just coincidence that a cross-section of the planet Earth looks remarkably like a cross-section of a baseball? Or is it further evidence that baseball is a part of the human soul?

Both the planet and the ball have a solid inner core, surrounded by several layers of less dense material. The Earth's lower and upper mantle (See, they even *named* it after a ballplayer!) correspond roughly to the hundreds of yards of yarn that are wrapped around a ball.

Finally, Earth and ball are sealed with crust and cowhide cover. Both

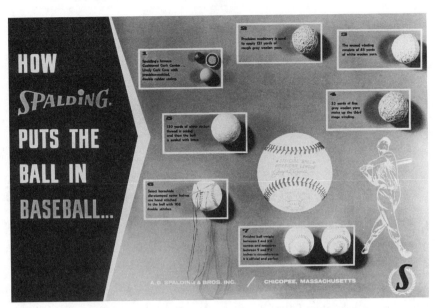

Figure 4-11 *(National Baseball Library, Cooperstown, NY)*

Figure 4-12A *(Rawlings Sporting Goods)*

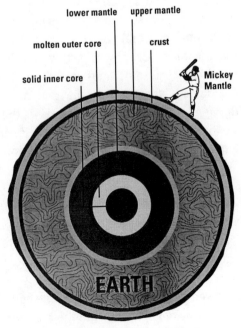

Figure 4-12B *(Nina Wallace)*

rotate, though the Earth's crust, as far as scientists have determined, is not held on by stitches. If it were, Earth would certainly *curve* through space, a hurtling breaking ball on an elliptical orbit to doomsday.

THE MAKING OF A BALL

You can't take a tour of the factory where Rawlings makes official major league baseballs. For one thing, it's in Costa Rica. For another, the process of making a ball is top secret. The following is a general description of how a baseball is manufactured. If you want to know more, tear the cover off a ball and unwind the insides.

▶ **The Pill.** *Figure 4-13* The first step is the "pill," the core of the ball. It's a little smaller than a golf ball. The pill is made of composition cork from Portugal surrounded by a thin layer of black-and-red rubber from southeast Asia.

▶ **The Cover.** *Figure 4-14* The cover of the ball is made in the U.S.A. The thin, lightweight hide of a midwestern Holstein cow is tanned, finished, cut, and punched with holes in the Rawlings plant in Tullahomma, Tennessee (though this photo is from the Spalding days).

Baseball assembly used to be an American operation, but part of the manufacturing process was moved to Haiti in 1973. During this period, baseballs were sometimes called "voodoo balls."

Political instability in Haiti prompted Rawlings to move baseball production to calmer shores. Nowadays, the pills and covers are shipped to Costa Rica for assembly. There, the innards of the ball are stored under strictly controlled temperature conditions.

▶ **The Yarn.** *Figures 4-15A, B* Baseballs are filled primarily with woolen yarn, because that material is resilient enough to compress when hit by a wooden bat and then return to its original shape. A machine winds 300 yards of blue-gray woolen yarn around the pill, followed by a thin layer of white yarn and another layer of blue-gray yarn. This is followed by a very thin layer of fine cotton yarn.

The tricky part is to wind the ball with a constant tension. Otherwise, the ball will be misshapen and have soft spots.

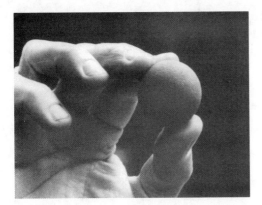

Figure 4-14 *(National Baseball Library, Cooperstown, NY)*

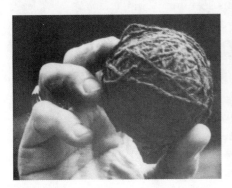

Figure 4-15A *(Collection of Bill Jaspersohn)*   **Figure 4-15B** *(Collection of Bill Jaspersohn)*

Figure 4-16 *(National Baseball Library, Cooperstown, NY)*

▲ **The Weigh-In.** *Figure 4-16* By this time, the ball should be 8.5 inches in circumference and weigh four and one-eighth ounces. If it's more than a fraction of an inch or ounce off, it's rejected.

▶ **Wrap It Up.** *Figures 4-17A, B* If you want to become a multimillionaire, invent a contraption that will sew a cover on a baseball. With all the fantastic machines humankind has been able to create, nobody has ever made one that can perform this seemingly simple task.

Instead, hundreds of workers in a factory do it by hand, the same way they've done it for a hundred years (Which is one big reason why baseball production was shifted to Latin America. Why pay workers $10 an hour when you can pay them $5 a day?).

The ball is mounted on a viselike device and waxed cotton thread is pulled through the holes in the cover. Until 1934, the American League used red and black thread while the National League used red and blue. Today, the thread is all red.

The "seams" on a baseball are actually one continuous seam held together by 108 stitches (softballs have 88). The reason you don't see the

Figure 4-17A *(National Baseball Library, Cooperstown, NY)*

Figure 4-17B *(Rawlings Sporting Goods)*

beginning or end of the thread is that the first and last stitches have been skillfully hidden. Using a needle, ball stitchers pull the thread through the last hole and push the needle until it comes out about ten seams away. Then they snip the thread and poke any excess under the seam. Altogether, it takes about 15 minutes to sew a ball.

▼ *Figure 4-18*   Finally the ball is rolled for about 15 seconds to compress the stitches and stamped:

Rawlings
OFFICIAL BALL
AMERICAN LEAGUE
Gene Budig, PRES.
CUSHIONED CORK CENTER
RO-N

The mysterious letters "RO" on baseballs are Rawlings' code to indicate the ball is the company's major league model. Much like minor league prospects, only about one out of three baseballs is considered good enough to see action in the big leagues.

After all that, the average life of a major league baseball is often as brief as one pitch, fouled into the stands. Umpires dole out as many as 50 balls in a single game. Rawlings delivers about 60,000 dozen balls for major league use through each regular season.

▶ **The Torture Chamber.**   *Figure 4-19*   Further testing goes on at the Rawlings "torture chamber" in Missouri. There, engineers shoot

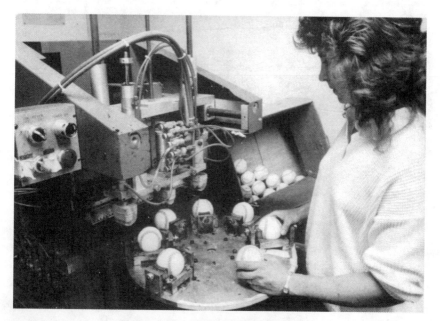

Figure 4-18   *(Collection of Bill Jaspersohn)*

Figure 4-19　*(Rawlings Sporting Goods)*

baseballs out of cannons at a wooden target eight feet away. A ball shot at 85 miles per hour should rebound at 54.6 percent of that velocity. If it's 3.2 percent higher or lower than that, the ball is not sent to the major leagues.

At the torture chamber, baseballs are also pounded 200 times and squeezed with 65 pounds of pressure. They pass the test if they distort less than .08 of an inch.

▶ **Mystery Mud.**　*Figure 4-20*　Before every major league game, the umpires smear a mildly abrasive mud on the baseballs. It removes the shine, raises the grain of the leather, and makes it easier to grip the ball—yet it doesn't darken or scratch it. This mud is the only substance in the world that can do that.

The mud is called "Lena Blackburne Baseball Rubbing Mud," after the man who discovered it along the Delaware River near his New Jersey home in the 1920s. Lena "Slats" Blackburne was a utility infielder who played on and off from 1910 to 1920, mostly for the Chicago White Sox. He managed the Sox in 1928 and 1929.

Only a few people know exactly where to find "Lena Blackburne Baseball Rubbing Mud." Blackburne revealed its exact location only to

Figure 4-20   *(National Baseball Library, Cooperstown, NY)*

his family. He would go out at night in a rowboat and scoop the stuff up. Then he'd mix it with some other mysterious substance and pack it in containers to ship out to major league teams.

Lena Blackburne cornered the mud market. He died in Riverside, New Jersey, in 1968. His family is still in the business. A can of mud costs $75.

▲ **Colored Balls.**   Most fans think that Oakland A's owner Charlie "I'll Try Anything" Finley introduced yellow and orange baseballs to the world in 1973. In fact, colored baseballs were used a hundred years before Finley bought his first can of Day-Glo paint.

In 1870, New York sporting goods company Peck & Snyder ran the following ad for their "Dead Red Ball": "Our new Ball is made of the best yarn, covering an ounce and a half of the best Unvulcanized Rubber, and is of a Dark Red color, thereby getting rid of the objectionable dazzling whiteness of the ordinary ball which bothers fielders and batsmen on a Sunny Day."

The 1938 Brooklyn Dodgers experimented with yellow baseballs during one night game. The idea was dropped when all the pitchers came off the mound with yellow fingers.

▼ **The Balata Ball.**   *Figure 4-21*   In the middle of World War II, the best rubber was needed for military purposes. Baseball was forced to search for a substitute that could be used around the cork center of the ball. A South American rubberlike gum called "balata" was chosen. It was similar to the covering of golf balls. In this photo, baseball commissioner Landis (center) examines the makings of balata balls to be used for the 1943 season.

The balata ball, unfortunately, was deader than the deadest dead ball. One month into the season, only two home runs had been hit by the entire American League. Hitler or no Hitler, rubber was put back into baseballs. The day it returned, six homers were slugged.

PS: We won the war anyway.

Figure 4-21   *(National Baseball Library, Cooperstown, NY)*

▼ **The Curvingest Ball in the World.**   *Figures 4-22A, B, C, D*   The Wiffle® Ball was invented in 1953 by Dave Mullany (right), a 44-year-old Fairfield, Connecticut, automobile polish salesman. His 12-year-old son, Dave Jr. (left), loved to play baseball with his friends. But the family backyard was too small for hardball, and the local playgrounds and schoolyards weren't much better.

"We started breaking windows," says Dave Jr. today, "and we just got kicked out of every place we could play."

Another problem was that he couldn't seem to get the hang of throw-

Figure 4-22A   *(The Wiffle® Ball)*

ing a curveball. His dad was concerned that practicing the pitch for hours would damage Dave's arm.

A Coty perfume factory was nearby, and the senior Mullany got a bunch of plastic half-sphere shells that were used as cosmetic cases for a Coty Christmas package. He sat down at his kitchen table with a razor blade and began slicing holes in the shells, figuring that the wind whistling through a ball might upset the aerodynamics enough to make for some interesting curves.

Mullany cut up each shell, then glued two halves together. He sent Dave Jr. and his friend "Rubber John" Bellus out into the backyard to test the ball. After a few hours of experimentation, all agreed that the model with eight oblong holes evenly spaced on one half curved best. In fact, it curved so well, the real skill came in trying to throw the thing *straight*.

Figure 4-22B   *(The Wiffle® Ball)*

CURVE   STRAIGHT   SLIDER

Figure 4-22C   *(The Wiffle® Ball)*

During their experimentation, when one of the boys struck out the other, he would shout "I whiffed you!" An American classic was born.

The auto polish firm went belly up and Dave Mullany couldn't land another job, so he put up his house as collateral to get a loan and formed The Wiffle® Ball, Inc., in his garage. "What the hell," he told Dave Jr. "If it'll keep you rotten kids that busy for so many hours, there must be something to it."

Within a year, the Wiffle® Ball took off. Millions of them have been sold in the four decades since then, and the company does absolutely no advertising. They have experimented with a Wiffle® football and a Wiffle® basketball, but neither has been successful. Dave Mullany passed away in 1990, and the president of The Wiffle® Ball, Inc., today is Dave Jr.

About 100 Wiffle® Balls roll off the assembly line in Shelton, Connecticut, every minute. One machine melts polyethylene beads and shapes them by injection molding into a half-sphere. Another welds the two halves together. The excess plastic is trimmed off by a human being. Rejected balls are melted again.

The Wiffle® Ball, Inc., has resisted expansion or buyouts, continuing to run simply with three machines in a factory the size of a four-car garage. The balls, which are made of "pure virgin plastic," were introduced at 49 cents back in 1954. They are still under a buck today. The Wiffle® Ball looks as if it's here for the long haul—Dave Mullany Jr.'s son works for the company, and *his* name is Dave too.

Notice that the original patent for the Wiffle® Ball indicates the inventor was W. F. Blamey, Jr., not Dave Mullany. William Blamey was Mullany's brother-in-law, a real-estate salesman and part-time tap dancer who loaned Mullany seed money to get Wiffle® Ball off the ground. Mullany was at work the day Blamey filed the patent application—under his *own* name.

"He had so many scams running," Dave Jr. says, "my dad was lucky to get away from him with his skin." Mullany later bought out Blamey.

Coincidentally, *another* salesman from the auto polish company, Peter Hodgson, was the genius behind another classic toy—Silly Putty. Hodgson was *also* inspired by the perfume containers at the Coty factory, which he used to make the toy's distinctive egg-shaped container.

It is a myth, by the way, that The Wiffle® Ball, Inc., mixes dogfood in with the plastic to increase sales of Wiffle® Balls. Dogs simply love chasing and gnawing on the things.

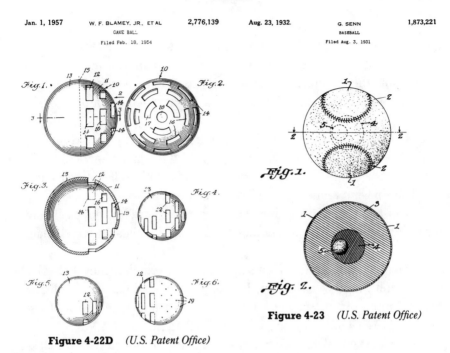

Jan. 1, 1957   W. F. BLAMEY, JR., ET AL   2,776,139   Aug. 23, 1932.   G. SENN   1,873,221

GAME BALL   BASEBALL

Filed Feb. 18, 1954   Filed Aug. 3, 1931

Figure 4-23   *(U.S. Patent Office)*

Figure 4-22D   *(U.S. Patent Office)*

▲ **The Wobble Ball.**   *Figure 4-23*   Inventor George Senn of Green Bay, Wisconsin, came up with another way for amateurs to throw curveballs. He moved the core of the ball (5) to one side to make the ball unbalanced.

"In consequence of this construction the center of gravity is offset from the true center of the ball and consequently allows the ball to be thrown with slightly greater curves than a conventional ball having the center of gravity at the true center of the baseball."

Senn, who may have been unbalanced himself, considered this an improvement to baseball because it would require players to be "more expert" at catching and hitting the ball.

▲ **The Optical Illusion Ball.**   For decades after it was invented, physicists and other disbelievers argued that the curveball didn't really curve. It was merely an optical illusion.

To settle the issue, in 1941 *Life* magazine hired world-renowned high-speed photography expert Gjon Mili to provide visible proof that a curve curved. Mili set up three synchronized cameras in a darkened room, with Hall of Fame pitcher Carl Hubbell throwing curveball after curveball. The cameras fired at one-thirtieth of a second intervals.

The results: "Possibly there is an infinitely small side movement of the ball, but these pictures fail to show it," reported *Life* in its September 15, 1941, issue. "This standby of baseball is after all only an optical illusion."

Baseball didn't buy it (especially the hitters who had to face Hubbell). In the late 1940s, Igor Sikorsky, who pioneered the invention of the helicopter, made it his mission to solve the riddle himself. Sikorsky put baseballs in wind tunnels to see if they could curve.

"It can be definitely concluded that a pitched baseball does actually curve," he concluded, "in addition to any optical illusion which may exist."

Twelve years after *Life* magazine's first experiment, they had Mili photograph the curveball again. This time he painted half the ball black to get a more distinct image. Cincinnati Reds left-hander Ken Raffensberger (119–154 lifetime) threw the crooked pitch.

"Yes, a curve ball does curve," *Life* announced this time. The magazine calculated that a typical curve spun at a rate of 1,400 revolutions per minute. (The problem is keeping the damn thing in the *air* for a minute.)

Any bumpkin ballplayer had known all along that the curve was no optical illusion, of course. Cincinnati manager Luke Sewell summed up baseball's position simply: "Isn't it strange that the optical illusion only happens when someone tries to throw a curveball, and never when a fast or straight ball is attempted?"

Today, any physicist is happy to tell you that baseballs curve because the spin creates a difference in air pressure on the two sides of the ball. According to Bernoulli's principle, the ball moves in the direction of least pressure. But scientists are still breaking baseball's balls. Now players and physicists argue about whether or not a fastball can actually *rise*.

▶ **The Safe Ball.** *Figure 4-24*   The leading cause of injury in baseball is being hit by the ball, especially in the head. A baseball traveling 60 mph that strikes a person's head will result in a serious injury 90 percent of the time.

The ball in this patent is called RIF, for "Reduced Injury Factor." Its core is made of molded polyurethane foam instead of cork. The ball

U.S. Patent   Aug. 24, 1976   3,976,295

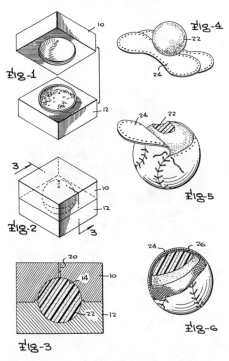

Figure 4-24   *(U.S. Patent Office)*

looks, feels, bounces, and sounds just like a regular baseball, but the chance of serious injury when one is hit in the head drops to 5 to 10 percent with a RIF ball.

The inventor of the RIF ball was Jess Heald, pioneer of the aluminum bat (see Chapter 1). Critics have argued that aluminum bats are dangerous because baseballs rocket off them so hard. It makes sense that Heald would design a ball that doesn't cause too much damage upon impact.

▶ **The Rise of Al Spalding.**   *Figures 4-25A, B*   On February 2, 1876, the National League was founded. The very next day, A. G. Spalding & Bros. was founded. It was not a coincidence.

Albert Goodwill Spalding was baseball's first great pitcher, and its first 200-game winner. He was spectacular in 1875, winning 56 games and losing just 4. He was pretty good with the bat too, hitting .318. At the

Yours Truly
A.G. Spalding

Figure 4-25A   *(Official Base Ball Guide)*

age of 26 and at the height of his career, he abruptly gave up playing so he could begin building his empire.

Al and his younger brother Walter borrowed $800 from their mother to open a small store at 118 Randolph Street in Chicago. Harriet Spalding not only put up the cash, she also helped sew team names on uniforms. Mary Spalding, Al's sister, served as the company bookkeeper.

The business was a good bet. The Civil War had spread baseball across America and there were a lot of young men out there in need of bats and balls. Just a year earlier a St. Louis first baseman named Charles Waite had had the audacity to appear on the field with a *glove* on his hand (see next chapter). Scandalous! Spalding, by then the most famous player in the game, started wearing a glove—and selling them, too.

Before long, the company was also selling bats, balls, sliding pads, masks, shoes, seat cushions, and other baseball paraphernalia. Al skillfully capitalized on his reputation as a famous player to launch the company. He was as shrewd on the business field as he had been on the baseball field. He moved to first base, keeping his face before the public every day.

The newly formed National League needed baseballs, and Spalding offered to provide them for free. In fact, his company *paid* the league one dollar for every dozen balls used. In return, A. G. Spalding & Bros. was granted the right to call *their* baseball the "official ball" of the National League. With that endorsement, Spalding marketed the ball to every team and boy in America who wanted to use the ball the pros used.

Spalding was also granted a monopoly to publish the National League's official guide, which he used to promote Spalding products

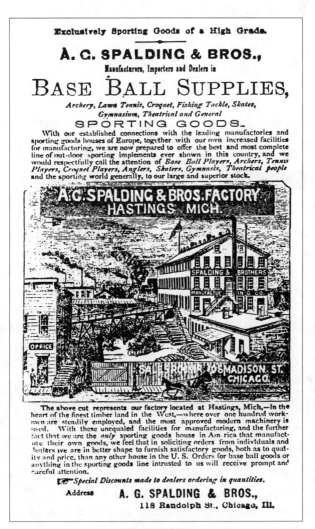

Figure 4-25B

and his own opinions. Soon the annual *Spalding Base Ball Guide* was selling 50,000 copies yearly. In case anybody wondered if he was ambitious, Al also secured the contract to make all the uniforms for the National League.

The business was booming. Al played just one game in 1878, then retired as a player to concentrate on the business full-time.

He bought his first factory in 1879 (figure 4-25B), and it was quickly turning out a million bats a year, as well as golf clubs, ice skates, tennis racquets, dumbbells, Indian clubs, bicycles, hunting equipment, every type of athletic gear imaginable. The company published 300 booklets on sport and health. For 25 cents, you could find out "How to Live 100 Years." Al Spalding's motto was: "Everything is possible to him who dares."

Unlike his competitors Reach and Shibe, Spalding never invented anything. He *paid* inventors so he could market their products. Spalding bought out the inventor of Bright's Baseball Turnstiles, Gray's Patented Chest Protector, and Decker's Safety Catching Mitt. When catcher's mask inventor Fred Thayer took his first mask to Wright & Ditson to manufacture, Spalding had a knockoff available within the year. When James Naismith invented a new game called "basketball" in 1894, it was Spalding he approached to design the game's official ball.

Spalding had an insatiable ego, and he was not above using unscrupulous tactics to drive a competitor or rival league out of business. One by one he swallowed up his competitors Peck & Snyder (1894), A. J. Reach Company (1889), and Wright & Ditson (1891).

Spalding's New York office opened in 1884, and three years later the company had its tentacles in 23 cities. Al took a bunch of players on a round-the-world tour in 1889, ostensibly to spread the joy of baseball globally. The group played a game in front of the Sphinx, and naturally it wasn't long before A. G. Spalding & Bros. had an office in Cairo.

By 1910, Al Spalding had accomplished more than he had ever dreamed possible. He ran for the Senate in California that year, but lost. He died five years later at the age of 65. When the Baseball Hall of Fame was established in 1939, one of the first inductees was Al Spalding.

Today, Spalding remains a force in the sporting world, with executive offices everywhere from Australia to New Zealand. When it comes to baseball, however, the company has been leapfrogged by Rawlings, Hillerich & Bradsby, and younger upstarts. In the current Spalding catalog, you have to page through footballs, basketballs, soccer balls, volleyballs, and even *jump ropes* before you reach a bat, baseball, or glove.

5

Protective Gear

It is estimated by an able statistician that the annual number of accidents caused by baseball in the last ten years has been 37,518, of which 3 per cent have been fatal; 25,611 fingers and 11,016 legs were broken during the decade in question, while 1,900 eyes were permanently put out and 1,648 ribs were fractured.

—The New York Times, *1881*

▶ *Figure 5-1* Baseball is a contact sport, and the contact was a lot more painful in the days before gloves, masks, helmets, and other protective gear became standard equipment. Before the 1880s, ballplayers wore no protection. A fractured rib or battered face was considered to be just a nuisance of the game, like rain delays. (Of course, if they didn't play, they didn't get paid.) Today, when players walk out on the field in a suit of armor, it seems as if half the league is on the disabled list at any given time.

▶ *Figures 5-2A, B* Catchers endure more punishment than any other position player. Before there was protective equipment, baseball teams would have one pitcher and a rotation of *catchers* to spread the pain around.

"He played with his right eye almost knocked out of his head," *The New York Times* wrote about New York Mutuals catcher Nat Hicks in 1873. "His nose and the whole right side of his face swollen three times normal size." Shaking hands with a catcher, it was said, was like grabbing a handful of walnuts.

Yankee catcher Bill Dickey dubbed catching gear "the tools of ignorance," which suggested that anyone with a brain in his head would

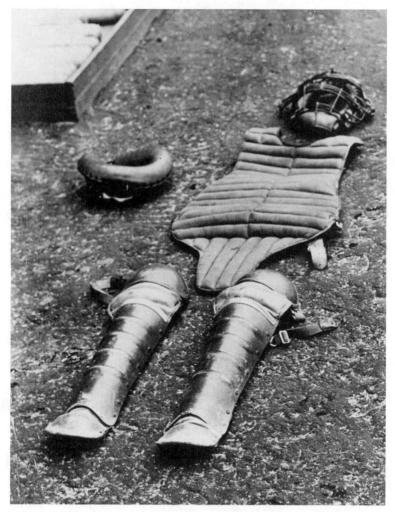

Figure 5-1   *(National Baseball Library, Cooperstown, NY)*

choose another position. We can only guess what they thought of catchers before these tools were available.

The first protective device specifically for baseball players was this 50-cent catcher's mouthpiece. It was invented in the 1860s by Hall of Famer George Wright (next page). Wright was a star on the Cincinnati Red Stockings, the first all-professional team, which was formed by his brother Harry.

The rubber mouth protector was intended to replace the thick rubber bands that some catchers wore around their heads to ward off flying balls and bats. The selling point was that "it can be held in the mouth without having any disagreeable taste."

George Wright was a clever baseball innovator in several respects. He figured out that if there was a runner on first, he could deliberately let an infield fly drop and turn it into a double play. This practice led to the infield fly rule. He is also credited with inventing batting practice. Hitters used to warm up by hitting fungoes until Wright thought of hitting pitched baseballs.

Wright was the first hitter in the history of the National League. Leading off for the Red Stockings on April 22, 1876, he grounded out to

Figure 5-2A
(National Baseball Library, Cooperstown, NY)

Figure 5-2B

short. After his playing days, he became the only man to ever win a pennant in his only year as a manager.

"We didn't need them in our day," sneered Wright when gloves and masks became part of the game. But in his day, most catchers were toothless and crippled in their twenties. George Wright, it should be noted, played shortstop, out of harm's way.

▼ **The Catcher's Mitt.** *Figure 5-3* Hall of Famer Buck Ewing *popularized* the catcher's mitt, but you can take your pick among the theories of who was the first catcher to wear one. It may have been Cincinnati Red Stocking Doug Allison (seen here), who supposedly had a saddle-maker sew him buckskin mittens in 1869. It may have been Jim White in 1872, who three years later would become the first catcher to take a position right behind the batter. It may have been William "Gunner" Mc-Gunnigle of Fall River, Massachusetts, who reportedly cut the fingers off a pair of bricklayers' gloves and wore them in an 1875 game. Or maybe it was New Orleans catcher Henry Fabian, who, in 1880, used two gloves on one hand with a piece of lead in the middle. In any case, by 1890 most catchers were wearing mitts.

Legend has it that catchers once put raw steaks in their mitts to absorb the impact of the speeding baseball. There is no documentation of whether the padding became part of the postgame dinner spread.

Figure 5-3 *(George Brace)*

▲ **Hints from Henry.** *"The catcher will find it advantageous, when facing swift pitching, to wear tough leather gloves, with the fingers cut off near the joint, as they will prevent his having his hands split and puffed up"* (Henry Chadwick, early baseball writer).

▼ *Figure 5-4* Despite his contempt for protective equipment, George Wright would go on to make a healthy living *selling* it to the growing legions of baseball players. Fielders were sometimes referred to as "catchers" in the 1800s, so it is not certain that the gloves in this 1879 ad qualify as catcher's mitts.

▼ *Figures 5-5A, B* After breaking two fingers, Providence player Arthur Irwin (seen here in a Philadephia uniform) had New Hampshire glove manufacturer Draper & Maynard pad a buckskin glove and sew

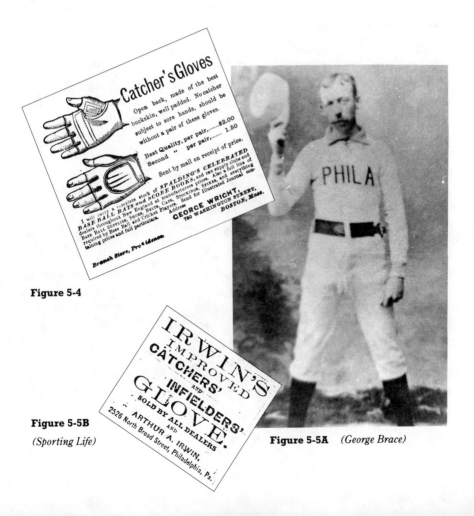

Figure 5-4

Figure 5-5B

(Sporting Life)

Figure 5-5A　*(George Brace)*

the two broken fingers together. It wasn't long before catchers all over the country were sporting "D & M" mitts. This ad appeared in an 1887 issue of *Sporting Life*. As far as I have been able to tell, it is the first documented case of a mitt specifically for catching.

▼ *Figure 5-6*   Joseph Gunson, catcher for the Kansas City Blues of the Western League, most often receives credit for inventing the catcher's mitt. On Decoration Day in 1888, Gunson was called on to catch a doubleheader despite having a severely banged-up finger.

"I stitched together the fingers of my left hand glove, thus practically making a mitt; and then I caught both games," Gunson said later. "It worked so well that I got to work, took an old paint-pot wire handle, the old flannel belts from our castoff jackets, rolled the cloth around the ends of the finger, and padded the thumb. Then I put sheepskins with the wool on it in the palm and covered it with buckskin, thus completing the mitt, and the suffering and punishment we endured at the then 50 foot pitching distances was all over."

Gunson and a teammate named Jimmy Manning intended to patent the invention, but Manning went on Al Spalding's world baseball tour in 1889 and never got around to it. Instead, Harry Decker (see below) reaped the financial rewards of the catcher's mitt.

PHILADELPHIA, PA., JULY 24, 1889.

J. B. GUNSON,
Tho Rising Young Catcher of the Kansas City Club.

Figure 5-6   *(Sporting Life)*

"However, I have received credit for being the real inventor," Gunson said. "I have a lifetime pass and I attend a great number of games accompanied by my wife. So I have much for which to be thankful." He passed away in 1942.

▼ **Deckers.** *Figures 5-7A, B, C* The first "modern" padded catcher's mitt was designed and patented in 1889 by Harry Decker, an infielder, outfielder, and catcher who played for many teams.

"In the modern game of base-ball it has become necessary for the 'catcher' to wear padded gloves for the protection of his hands to enable him to endure the swift and repeated blows of the ball," wrote Decker and his partner Paul Buckley. "The object of our invention is to provide a catcher's glove in which the padding shell shall be so arranged or distributed as to present greater relative thicknesses in certain determinate parts of the glove than in others."

Decker claimed the danger of breaking a finger in his glove was "greatly reduced, if not rendered practically impossible."

In the first Decker ad, the beginnings of the padded mitt with a primitive "pocket" can be seen. In the later ad, from 1907, the Decker truly resembles a modern catcher's mitt.

Spalding purchased the rights to market the Decker Patent Safety Catcher's Mitt, and for a time catcher's mitts were called "deckers."

The Baseball Encyclopedia lists Harry Decker simply as "deceased." No year, no location.

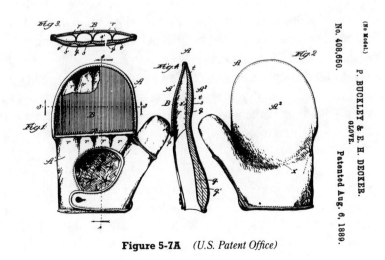

Figure 5-7A *(U.S. Patent Office)*

Figure 5-7B

"Decker Patent" Mitt

Face, sides and finger-piece of velvet tanned brown leather and back of selected buck; well padded and double row of stitching on heel pad, with the addition of a heavy piece of sole leather on back for extra protection to the hand and fingers; strap-and-buckle fastening at back; reinforced and laced at thumb, and made with our patent laced back.

No. OX.
Each, $3.50
Made in Rights and Lefts.

No. OX

Showing Back of No. OX Mitt

A. G. SPALDING & BROS.
Send for Complete Catalogue of all Athletic Sports. | Stores in all large cities. See inside cover page of this book.

Decker Patent Safety Catcher's Mitt.

Decker Mitt, Front.

Decker Throwing Glove to go with Mitt.

Decker Safety Catching Mitt, Back.

We take pleasure in calling attention to the new Decker Safety Catching Mitt, which has wherever shown and introduced, been conceded to be unequaled for protection to the hands. A catcher need have no fear of broken fingers when wearing them. Price per pair, $5 00.
Each pair is packed in a separate box.

Figure 5-7C

▶ **Catcher's Mitts Circa 1910.** *Figures 5-8A, B* Mitts became larger, especially as pitchers developed knuckleballs, spitballs, sliders, and other baffling breaking pitches.

They reached ridiculous proportions in the late 1950s. Baltimore catchers were having a helluva time handling Hoyt Wilhelm's knuckleball (Ray Katt allowed four passed balls in one disastrous inning). Baltimore Manager Paul Richards had Wilson Sporting Goods create "Big Bertha"—a mitt that appeared to be the size of a garbage can cover.

At the time nobody had bothered writing a rule that limited the size of a glove. Since then somebody has. Today, catcher's mitts cannot exceed 38 inches in circumference.

▲ In the 1950s, journeymen catcher Gus Niarhos cut an opening in the back of his mitt so he could squeeze the two sides together a little bit, like a fielder's glove. This led to catcher's mitts with breaks in them and one-handed catching, which would be popularized by Johnny Bench.

Figure 5-8A

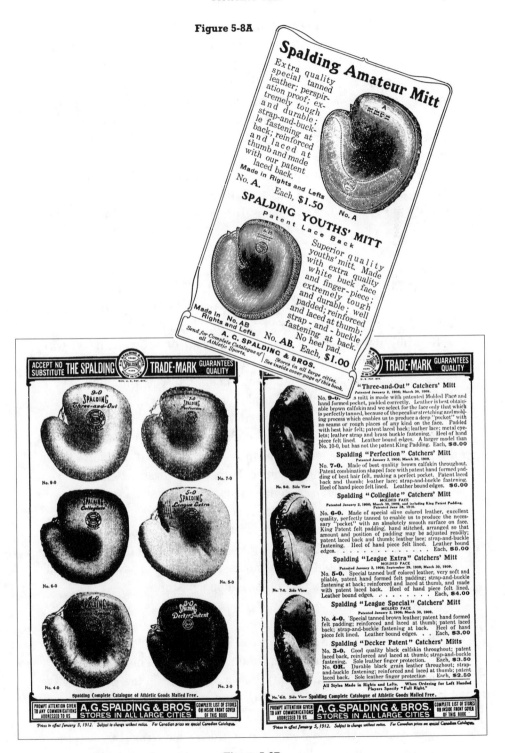

Figure 5-8B

▶ **The Glow-in-the-Dark Mitt.** *Figure 5-9* And you thought Al Campanis didn't have the *necessities* to be an inventor! Before he was thrown out of baseball in 1987 for making racist remarks on the television show *Nightline,* Campanis patented a mitt with a strip of fluorescent orange around the perimeter to help pitchers concentrate on the target.

"Normally, the entire glove, and particularly the entire catching side of the glove, is made of a relatively dull, substantially nonreflective color, ranging from tan to dark brown," wrote Campanis. "Such a catching side or surface provides a poor 'target' for a throwing player, and particularly a pitcher, to concentrate on in throwing a baseball to the player wearing the glove." The Campanis Target Mitt was marketed by Rawlings.

▶ **Look Ma, No Mitt!** *Figures 5-10A, B* There's no rule that says you have to catch with a glove on your hand. In 1904, an Illinois man named James E. Bennett came up with this alternative.

Basically, it was a sort of chicken coop made of wood and heavy wire that the catcher would strap to his chest. The two doors could be swung open. When a ball went through the opening, it would thump a pad at the rear and drop through a tube into the catcher's waiting hand.

"My invention relates to certain new and useful improvements in devices to be used by catchers and other players to protect their hands, the same being so constructed as to receive and retain the ball without the players' hands coming in contact therewith," insisted Bennett.

The Cincinnati Enquirer commented: "Mr. Bennett's catcher resembles a cage built for a homesick bear or a dyspeptic hyena."

On a high pop, presumably, the catcher would have to run to the spot where he judged the ball was going to land, then lie on the ground face up and wait for it to hit him in the stomach. Needless to say, the baseball catcher did not become a part of the national pastime.

▶ **The Catcher's Mask.** *Figures 5-11A, B, C, D* The catcher's mask was invented because a man didn't want to spoil his looks.

James Alexander Tyng (right) was an outfielder on the Harvard Law School baseball team in 1877. One day the captain and third baseman of the team, Frederick Winthrop Thayer (left), asked Tyng to play catcher.

Tyng refused. He knew what happened to catchers. They lost their teeth. They had bruises all over their faces. Tyng didn't want to become

PATENTED AUG 1 2 1975   3,898,696   **Figure 5-9**   *(U.S. Patent Office)*

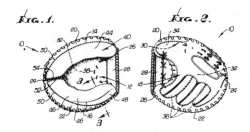

Fig. 1.   Fig. 2.

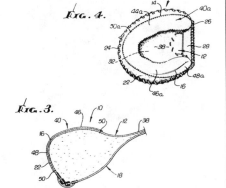

Fig. 4.

Fig. 3.

No. 755,209.   PATENTED MAR. 22, 1904.

J. E. BENNETT.
BASE BALL CATCHER.
APPLICATION FILED FEB. 18, 1903.

NO MODEL.   4 SHEET —SHEET 4.

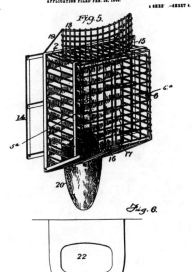

Fig. 5.

Fig. 6.

22

7

Figure 5-10A   *(U.S. Patent Office)*

A New Baseball Catcher

An ingenious apparatus shown in the accompanying illustration is intended to save the catcher's hands.

The doors on the front of the box are mounted to swing inwardly when the ball strikes them and the ball impacts against a padded cushion at the back of the box. After striking the cushion, the ball drops down and rolls through an opening at the lower part of the box.

Figure 5-10B   *(Cincinnati Enquirer)*

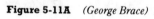

Figure 5-11A   *(George Brace)*   **Figure 5-11B**   *(George Brace)*

F. W. THAYER.
Masks.

No. 200,358.   Patented Feb. 12, 1878.

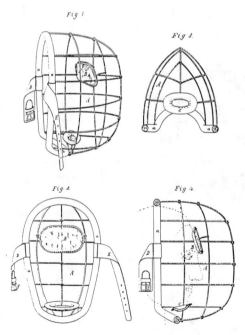

Figure 5-11C   *(U.S. Patent Office)*

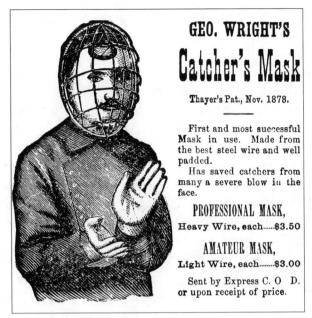

Figure 5-11D

disfigured. His family was opposed to the idea too. He told Thayer that if he was forced to catch, he would quit the team.

But James Tyng also loved baseball. So he proposed this compromise—if Thayer would get him a mask of some sort that would protect his face, he would take a stab behind the plate.

Thayer went to a wiremaker in Boston and had him construct a variation of a fencer's mask, made of meshed wire and cushioned with leather.

"It was not an infrequent occurrence in the game of baseball for a player to be severely injured in the face by a ball thrown against it," Thayer would write later. "It was up to me to devise some means of having the impact of the blow kept from driving the mask onto the face. The forehead and chin rest accomplished this and also made it possible for me to secure a patent, which I did in the winter of 1878."

On his patent application (left), Thayer said the purpose of his invention was to "protect the face of a player from being hit or injured by a base-ball while in flight toward him, and also at the same time to not materially obstruct his sight. It is usually to be worn by the catcher or person in rear of the striker or bat-wielder."

James Tyng tried the device for the first time in a game on April 12,

1877, against The Live Oaks, a local semipro team.* Harvard won 11–3 and Tyng committed only two errors, which was considered flawless fielding in his day.

The catcher's mask was met with scorn from opposing players and the press. One sportswriter commented, "There is a great deal of beastly humbug in contrivances to protect men from things which do not happen. There is about as much sense in putting a lightning rod on a catcher as there is a mask."

Another wrote: "We shall probably soon behold the spectacle of a player sculling around the bases with a stove funnel on his legs and a boiler-iron riveted across his stomach."

Thayer's invention was referred to as a "rat trap," a "muzzle," and most commonly, a "bird cage."

But catchers certainly appreciated it. Thayer took a prototype to Wright & Ditson, the Boston sporting goods firm established by George Wright. Wright agreed to manufacture the mask and pay Thayer a royalty for each one sold.

He sold plenty. By the early 1880s, catcher's masks were an accepted part of the uniform. Imitators rushed to sell competing masks, and Thayer, by then a Boston lawyer, would be busy for years in court defending his claim. In one celebrated 1886 case, he successfully sued Spalding for patent infringement. Nevertheless, Spalding marketed its own mask and warned customers that "cheap" versions from competitors were "worse than no protection at all" and were "liable to disfigure a player for life" (see the Spalding ad on page 188).

According to James Tyng, Thayer "made quite a large sum of money" from the invention of the catcher's mask. One of the original models can be seen at the Harvard Varsity Club in Cambridge, Massachusetts. Another is displayed in the Baseball Hall of Fame.

Before the invention of the catcher's mask, catchers positioned themselves about 10 feet behind home plate and caught pitches on a bounce. In 1880, it was ruled that third strikes had to be caught on a fly, giving catchers a reason to move forward. The catcher's mask gave them the courage to squat right behind the batter, where they could pay better attention to baserunners and become the generals who run the game on the field.

---

*Another Harvard catcher of the era, Howard K. Thatcher, claimed that *he* was the first to use Thayer's mask. Tyng and Thatcher had a spirited argument in the letters column of *The New York Sun* in 1896. Most histories of baseball credit Tyng as the first catcher to wear a mask.

▼ *Figure 5-12*   Frederick Thayer's original catcher's mask.

▼ **Or Is *This* the First Catcher's Mask?** *Figure 5-13* Aarne Anton, the curator of the American Primitive Gallery in New York, purchased this mask and displayed it in an exhibit of sporting equipment in 1993. It appears to be more primitive than Fred Thayer's mask, but there is no way of knowing when or where it was used.

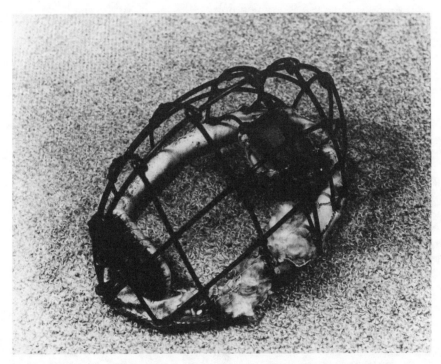

Figure 5-12   *(National Baseball Library, Cooperstown, NY)*

Figure 5-13   *(American Primitive Gallery, New York City)*

▼ **Why the Long Face?** *Figure 5-14* As with any new invention, improvements to the catcher's mask were proposed almost immediately. A few months after Thayer's patent, George Howland of Boston patented a mask with more padding for the chin and side of the head. In 1916 Brooklyn catcher Art Dede introduced his "platform mask" with two crossbars instead of wire mesh. Dede's entire big league career consisted of one game, in which he made one putout and had one turn at bat.

Three years after Thayer's first catcher's mask, ads such as this one were already calling it "the old style" mask. Notice that Spalding sold two versions of its mask—depending on the length of the catcher's face.

▼ **The Best Imported Dogskin.** *Figure 5-15* Albert Spalding never missed an opportunity to claim credit or disparage his competitors.

Figure 5-15

Spalding's Trade-Marked Catcher's Mask.

The first Catcher's Mask brought out in 1875, was a very heavy, clumsy affair, and it was not until we invented our open-eyed mask in 1877 that it came into general use. Now it would be considered unsafe and even dangerous for a catcher to face the swift underhand throwing of the present day unless protected by a reliable mask. The increased demand for these goods has brought manufacturers into the field who, having no reputation to sustain, have vied with each other to see how *cheap* they could make a so-called mask, and in consequence have ignored the essential qualification, *strength*. A cheaply made, inferior quality mask is much worse than no protection at all, for a broken wire or one that will not stand the force of the ball with caving in, is liable to disfigure a player for life. We would warn catchers not to trust their faces behind one of these cheaply made masks. Our trade-marked masks are made of the very best hard wire, plated to prevent rusting, and well trimmed, and every one is a thorough face protector. We shall make them in three grades as described below, and with our increased facilities for manufacturing, are enabled to improve the quality, and at the same time reduce the price.

Beware of counterfeits. *None genuine without our Trade Mark stamped on each Mask.*

No. 0. SPALDING'S SPECIAL LEAGUE MASK, used by all the leading professional catchers, extra heavy wire, well padded with goathair and the padding faced with the best imported dogskin, which is impervious to perspiration and retains its pliability and softness. .... Each. $3 00

No. 2. SPALDING'S AMATEUR MASK, made the same size and general style as the League Mask, but with lighter wire and faced with leather, (we guarantee this Mask to be superior to socalled professional Masks sold by other manufacturers)........................ 2 00

No. 3. SPALDING'S BOY'S MASK, similar to the Amateur Mask, only made smaller to fit a boy's face.................................. 1 75

☞ Any of these Masks mailed postpaid on receipt of price.

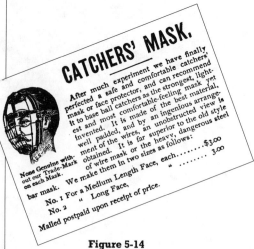

CATCHERS' MASK.

After much experiment we have finally perfected a safe and comfortable catchers' mask or face protector, and can recommend it to base ball catchers as the strongest, lightest and most comfortable-feeling mask yet invented. It is made of the best material, well padded, and by an ingenious arrangement of the wires, an unobstructed view is obtained. It is far superior to the old style of wire mask or the heavy, dangerous steel bar mask. We make them in two sizes as follows:

No. 1 For a Medium Length Face, each........$3.00
No. 2 " Long Face, " 3.00

Mailed postpaid upon receipt of price.

None Genuine with out our Trade-Mark on each Mask.

Figure 5-14

▼ **The Free-Spitting Mask.**   *Figure 5-16*   In 1923, James E. Johnstone of Newark, New Jersey, patented this one-piece metal shell that fit around the head and solved the age-old baseball dilemma of spitting through a mask. He wrote: "A large opening M may be provided immediately below the nose-bridge K and, in the interests of lightness and to permit free-spitting, may be made of ample proportions."

▼ **The Billy Goat.**   *Figure 5-17*   Los Angeles Dodger catcher Steve Yeager popularized the "billy goat" neck guard. In 1976 he was kneeling in the on-deck circle when a bat shattered and slammed into his throat. Yeager had nine splinters removed from his neck. But Yeager, who is the nephew of legendary jet pilot Chuck Yeager, was fearless. Soon he was back behind the plate, wearing this device.

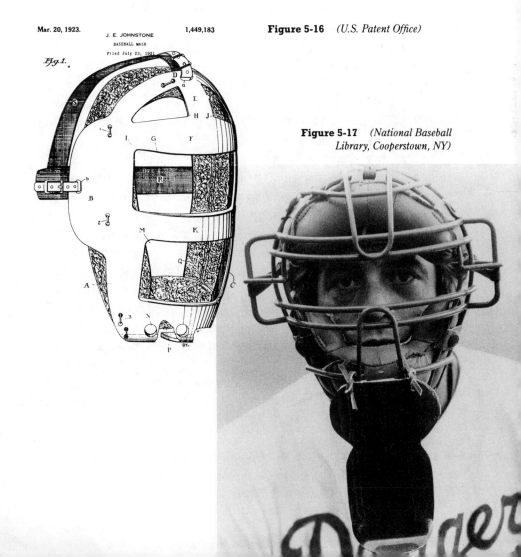

Mar. 20, 1923.

J. E. JOHNSTONE

BASEBALL MASK

Filed July 23, 1921

1,449,183

Figure 5-16   *(U.S. Patent Office)*

Fig.1.

Figure 5-17   *(National Baseball Library, Cooperstown, NY)*

▲ Despite the benefits of masks and mitts, some old-time catchers longed for the good old days when real men didn't need protective gear. George B. Ellard, who helped organize the Cincinnati Red Stockings in 1869, wrote this poem years later:

> We used not mattress on our hands
> Nor cage upon our face;
> We stood right up and caught the ball
> With courage and with grace.

▶ **The "Breast Protector."** *Figure 5-18* Once it became acceptable for catchers to wear protective devices on their hand and face, it didn't seem so outrageous when they began appearing on the field with protection over their upper body.

As with most baseball inventions, there is disagreement over who first wore a chest protector—or a "sheepskin," as it was first called. Some sources give credit to John T. Clements of the Philadelphia Keystones in the Union Association, who wore one in a game at Cincinnati in 1884. Clements, it is said, wore his chest protector beneath his uniform to avoid being called a sissy.

Others give credit to Detroit catcher Charles Bennett in 1886. Or rather, Charles Bennett's wife. The story goes that Mrs. Bennett would worry about her husband getting hit by pitches and foul tips, so she rigged up a device that covered his torso.

"In a private tryout it worked well and Charles, after permitting the ball to strike him repeatedly without feeling a jar, decided to use it in public," recalled a 1914 article in *Leslie's Weekly* magazine.

Chest protectors, sadly, protect only the chest. In 1894, Bennett's 15-year career was ended when he was run over by a Santa Fe passenger train in Kansas. Both his legs had to be amputated. Bennett is on the left in this 1916 photo with Billy Sunday and Sam Thompson, presumably wearing wooden legs.

Until he died in 1927, Charles Bennett appeared at the ballpark in Detroit on Opening Day to receive the traditional first pitch of the season.

▶ **Inflatables.** *Figure 5-19* Pneumatic bicycle tires had been invented in 1887 by Irishman John Dunlop, and air cushioning was tested

Figure 5-18 *(National Baseball Library, Cooperstown, NY)*

Figure 5-19

with all sorts of devices, including chest protectors. The most popular was the inflatable Gray's Patent Body Protector, seen in this 1889 ad.

Spalding marketed it, running ads showing a catcher doubled over in pain. "If only the poor lad had purchased any one of a number of models of Gray's Patented Catcher Protector, now manufactured exclusively by A. G. Spalding and Company, such fate could be avoided."

▶ *Figure 5-20*   Gray's Protector didn't cover the shoulders, a prime target for foul tips. Philadelphian John Gamble added inflatable pads that covered the catcher's shoulders and his protector was sold by Reach.

Later, sporting goods manufacturers would switch from air to a filling of kapok, a lightweight material used in life jackets. Today, chest protectors are filled with foam.

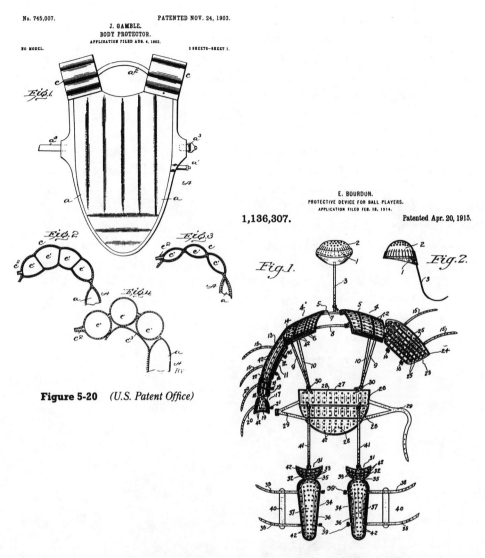

No. 745,007. PATENTED NOV. 24, 1903.
J. GAMBLE.
BODY PROTECTOR.
APPLICATION FILED AUG. 4, 1903.
NO MODEL. 2 SHEETS—SHEET 1.

Figure 5-20 *(U.S. Patent Office)*

E. BOURDON.
PROTECTIVE DEVICE FOR BALL PLAYERS.
APPLICATION FILED FEB. 18, 1914.
1,136,307. Patented Apr. 20, 1915.

Figure 5-21 *(U.S. Patent Office)*

▲ **The All-Purpose Protector.** *Figure 5-21* In 1914, Elie Bourdon of West Vancouver invented this mix-and-match contraption with removable padding. It could be adapted to any sport, depending on which part of the body was most likely to be injured.

Seventy years later, National League umpire Joe West invented the "West Vest," a protective vest that could be disassembled for portability and cleaning. West claimed his idea was stolen by Riddell Inc. and in 1993 filed a $10 million lawsuit. The West Vest is now manufactured by Douglas in Houston.

▼ **The Father of Shin Guards.** *Figure 5-22* "Every catcher in the business'll be wearing these things inside of six months." That's what New York Giant manager John McGraw said when his catcher Roger Bresnahan strapped on the first pair of shin guards in 1906. Other catchers had worn pads *under* their uniform pants, but it took tough-as-nails Bresnahan to have the nerve to admit publicly that his legs were killing him.

"I was sick and tired of wild pitches, foul balls, thrown bats, and flying spikes bruising and cutting my legs," Bresnahan said in a 1926 interview. "Boy, they sure called me a lot of names when I first put them on. But I guess they were a good idea; they tell me catchers still wear 'em."

Bresnahan, who was also the first major leaguer to try a batting helmet, is usually cited as the *inventor* of shin guards, but he never patented them or claimed credit for the innovation. "I didn't invent anything," he said. "I simply got a pair of shin guards, such as cricket players wore." Bresnahan was inducted into the Hall of Fame in 1945, a few months after he passed away. A pair of his shin guards is owned by

Figure 5-22   *(George Brace)*

Barry Halper, a New Jersey man whose baseball memorabilia collection rivals the Hall of Fame.

Nowadays, some hitters wear modified shin guards to protect their ankles and forearms from foul tips.

▲ **Fielders' Gloves.**　In the early 1870s, it was not unusual to see an outfielder circle under a high fly, take the cap off his head, and catch the ball in it. But around the same time catchers began wearing mitts, position players began wearing gloves.* Fielding gloves started out as a protective device, but evolved into an extension of the hand for better fielding.

"The first glove I ever saw on the hand of a ballplayer in a game," recalled Albert Spalding, "was worn by a first baseman named Charles C. Waite in Boston, in 1875. The glove worn by him was flesh color with a large round opening in back."

Waite's glove hasn't survived, but probably resembled today's work gloves. He chose a flesh-colored one in hope that fans and opposing players wouldn't notice. It didn't work. Waite was teased and mocked for being a sissy.

Two years later, Al Spalding's sporting goods company was thriving and he had switched to first base for his last season as an active player. To protect his hands (and perhaps have something new to sell to thousands of baseball players), Spalding began wearing a glove—a *black* one that stood out like, well, a sore thumb. Nobody was going to poke fun at Al Spalding, one of the biggest stars in the game. Following Spalding's lead, other players began wearing gloves. Still, it took nearly a decade for the glove to become accepted.

"The game of baseball is being spoiled by allowing players to wear these abominations known as mitts," complained a Boston player named Harry Schafer. "Players do not have to show skill in handling balls with those mitts in their hands. Those who cannot play without them should get out of the game and give way to those who can."

It would turn out to be the other way around.

▶ **The First Patent for a Baseball Glove.**　*Figures 5-23A, B*　Three years after Charles Waite wore the first glove on the field, Austin C.

---

*The difference between a mitt and a glove is that catchers and first basemen use mitts, while everybody else uses a glove.

Butts of Newark, New Jersey, patented a glove "for sporting and general use." It is not clear if that meant playing baseball, but in 1883 Butts was issued another patent for a fingerless glove clearly intended for sports.

"The glove shown and described is a short glove, such as is used by ball and cricket players for the purpose of protecting the hand," Butts wrote. He also patented a boxing glove in 1878.

▶ **George H. Rawlings.** *Figures 5-24A, B, C, D* Does the name look familiar? Rawlings, of St. Louis, patented this padded, short-fingered buckskin glove, which had two layers of felt with a layer of rubber between them. "The glove is intended especially for the use of base-ball players and cricketers," wrote Rawlings, "the pads being for the prevention of the bruising of the hands when catching the ball."

George and his brother Alfred formed a little company, and a century later Rawlings Sporting Goods makes the gloves for more than half of the players in the majors. The company is also the official supplier of major league baseballs. These ads from the late 1880s closely resemble the Rawlings patent.

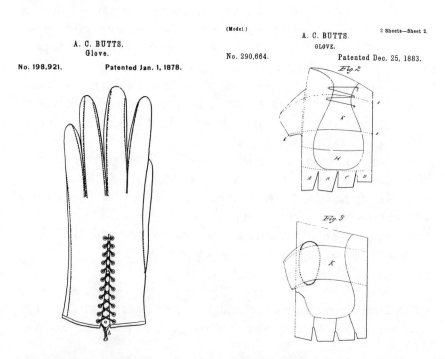

Figure 5-23A *(U.S. Patent Office)*   **Figure 5-23B** *(U.S. Patent Office)*

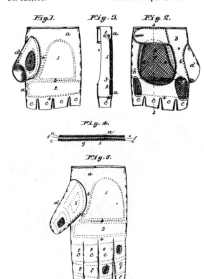

(No Model.)

G. H. RAWLINGS.

GLOVE.

No. 325,968.   Patented Sept. 8, 1885.

Figure 5-24A   *(U.S. Patent Office)*

Figure 5-24B   *(National Baseball Library, Cooperstown, NY)*

Reach's Catchers' Gloves.

This season we introduce for the first time our new Fielder's Full-Fingered Glove. This glove is specially designed for Fielder's use, it is made of the best buckskin and while heavily padded to prevent bruises, it is so soft and pliable that a player can pick up a ball as well with as without it. It is almost impossible to miss a fly ball while wearing it. All professionals are wearing the Fielder's Glove. Price, each, $3.50.

No. 000. Reach's Special Association Catchers' Gloves.

Full Left Hand, made of the best and heaviest mouse-   Per Pair.
colored buckskin. The full left hand glove with
or without sole leather finger tips. Extra thick
padding and lined with best Chamois Skin. The
Right Hand Glove is made without fingers, extra
padded,—the best Gloves made............... $5.00

No. 00. Reach's Association Catchers' Gloves.

Full Left hand, made of best mouse-colored buckskin, same as No. 000 gloves, but without sole leather tips and not lined. Right hand glove fingerless.................................... 3 50

No. 01. Reach's Full Left Hand Catchers' Gloves.

Made of heavy buckskin and well padded, equal to any glove in the market for the price......... 2.50

No. 02. Reach's Full Left Hand Catchers' Gloves.

Made of good quality, heavy leather.............. 1.2

Reach's Catchers' Gloves—Continued.

No. 0. Reach's Association Catchers' Gloves.

Made of extra heavy mouse-colored buckskin with-   Per Pair.
out fingers, open back, extra well padded and
warranted................................. $2.50

No. 1. Reach's Professional Catchers' Gloves.

Made of heavy buckskin, without fingers, open back and well padded............................. 2.00

No. 2. Reach's Amateur Gloves.

Made of good quality, heavy leather, open back and well padded.................................. 1.50

No. 3. Reach's Practice Gloves.

Made of light leather, open back and padded....... 1.00

No. 4. Junior Gloves.

Open back.... .... .50

No. 5. Cheap Gloves.

Open back..... .... .25

Any of the above gloves mailed, postpaid, upon receipt of price.
In ordering always state size of gloves worn.

Figure 5-24C

Figure 5-24D   *(Sporting Life)*

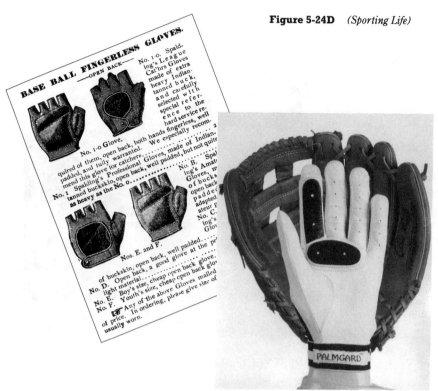

Figure 5-25   *(Palmguard International)*

▲ **Déjà Vu.**   *Figure 5-25*   The first gloves looked a bit like the gloves players wear *inside* their gloves today. Palmgard (seen here) was invented in 1988 by former Little League coach Charles Webster. The dark areas provide extra protection for the areas that sting the most when a ball is caught—the first finger and palm.

▶ **The Last Barehanders.**   *Figure 5-26*   Louisville third baseman Jeremiah Denny (next page) was the last position player to take the field without a glove. Denny was ambidextrous. He would pick up grounders with whichever hand was . . . handiest, and then throw to first base with that hand. Denny never had to backhand a ball, and apparently didn't want to learn. He retired after the 1894 season. *The Baseball Encyclopedia* lists Denny's lifetime fielding average as .890. Not bad for an era when making four errors in an inning was not uncommon.

The last pitcher to play without a glove was Gus Weyhing, who called it quits after the 1901 season.

Figure 5-26   *(George Brace)*

▲ **Tenney, Anyone?**   Around the turn of the century gloves were sometimes called "tenneys," after Fred Tenney, an excellent fielder (.982 lifetime) who used a fat, circular glove. Tenney, for what it's worth, is listed in *The Bill James Historical Baseball Abstract* as the ugliest player of the 1890s.

▶ **The Double Glove.**   *Figure 5-27*   Remember the cage built for the homesick bear on page 183? A year later, the same inventor came up with this brainstorm. James Bennett's idea was for the fielder to wear a glove on *each* hand, with a sheet of leather connecting them. When the ball landed in the middle, the two gloves would be drawn together to hold it tightly.

This glove probably came in handy for those cold October days, but picture an outfielder running after a fly ball with this thing on.

▶ **Famous Gloves.**   *Figure 5-28*   Bennett's double glove may have looked ridiculous, but it addressed a real problem—early baseball gloves had no *pocket*. The gloves in this photo belonged to (from left to

No. 789,480.

J. E. BENNETT.
BASE BALL GLOVE.
APPLICATION FILED DEC. 17, 1904.

PATENTED MAY 9, 1905.

2 SHEETS—SHEET 1.

Figure 5-27   *(U.S. Patent Office)*

Fig.1.

Fig.2.

Figure 5-28   *(National Baseball Library, Cooperstown, NY)*

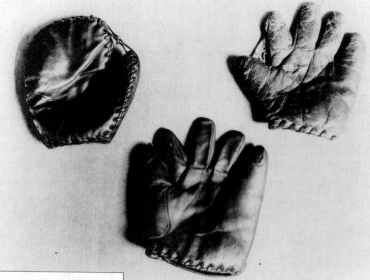

Spalding's No. 5X Fielders' Mitt

An exceedingly good mitt at a popular price; the face made of light tanned buckskin, brown leather back; laced thumb; constructed throughout in a most substantial manner.

No. 5X. Each, $1.00

Figure 5-29

right) first baseman George Sisler, Cy Young, and Christy Mathewson. Notice that the fingers of Young's and Mathewson's gloves are not laced together. The only way to hold on to a ball was to catch it right on the palm, which was difficult and painful.

▼ **The "Perfect" Glove.**   *Figure 5-30*   Fortunately, inventors did not stop trying to improve the baseball glove, despite this 1910 claim of achieved perfection.

▼ **Nothing to Spit At.**   *Figure 5-31A, B, C*   One day in 1919, St. Louis Cardinal pitcher "Spittin' Bill" Doak (seen here) had a brainstorm. If he attached a few strips of material between the thumb and first finger of his glove, Doak figured, it would form a pocket. He would be able to catch balls *away* from the sensitive palm of his hand, and make one-handed catches more easily.

The modern baseball glove was born. Doak patented his new glove

Figure 5-31A   *(George Brace)*

Figure 5-30

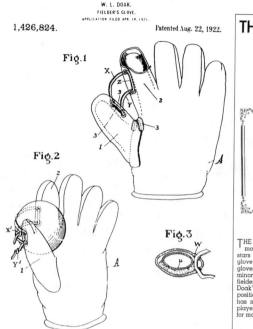

W. L. DOAK.
FIELDER'S GLOVE.
APPLICATION FILED APR. 19, 1921.

1,426,824.   Patented Aug. 22, 1922.

Fig.1

Fig.2

Fig.3

Figure 5-31B   *(U.S. Patent Office)*

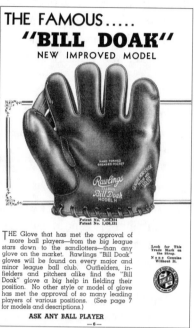

THE FAMOUS.....
"BILL DOAK"
NEW IMPROVED MODEL

Rawlings
Bill Doak
MODEL H

Patent No. 1,426,824
Patent No. 1,436,131

THE Glove that has met the approval of more ball players—from the big league stars down to the sandlotters—than any glove on the market. Rawlings "Bill Doak" gloves will be found on every major and minor league ball club. Outfielders, infielders and pitchers alike find the "Bill Doak" glove a big help in fielding their position. No other style or model of glove has met the approval of so many leading players of various positions. (See page 7 for models and descriptions.)

Look for This
Trade Mark on
the Strap.
None Genuine
Without It.

ASK ANY BALL PLAYER
— 6 —

Figure 5-31C   *(Rawlings Sporting
Goods Co.)*

and sold the rights to Rawlings. The $9 glove, which was named after its inventor, became a sensation.

The object of his invention, Doak wrote, was "to provide a fielder's glove in which the thumb and index finger of the glove are connected together by a plurality of strands that extend transversely across the space between the thumb and index finger and cooperate with said parts to form a pocket which will conform or adjust itself automatically to a ball caught by the glove."

Notice that on Doak's glove, only the thumb and first finger are connected.

Doak was nicknamed "Spittin' Bill" because he was a spitballer. When the pitch was banned in 1920, he was one of 18 pitchers who were permitted to keep throwing it until the end of their career. Doak retired in 1929, after winning 170 games and losing 157. He had two great seasons, 1914 (20–6, 1.72 ERA) and 1921 (15–6, 2.59 ERA).

Bill Doak did not become fabulously wealthy from his invention. He ran a candy store for many years in Bradenton, Florida, where he died in 1954.

▼ **The U Crotch, and Other Hits.** *Figures 5-32A,B,C* Bill Doak's revolutionary glove would be improved upon by other inventors, most notably Harry "The Glove Doctor" Latina. After his minor league career was ended by a broken ankle, Latina was hired by Rawlings to be the company's first glove designer. It was 1922—the same year Bill Doak received his patent. Over the next 40 years, Latina would receive more than 30 patents, three of which are reproduced here.

Sportswriter Red Smith once wrote that Harry Latina was "the man most responsible for the demise of the .400 hitter." Latina's greatest hits were the Deep Well Pocket (1940), the Trapper (1940), the U Crotch (1941), the Snugger Wrist Adjustment (1942), the Palm Crotch Extension (1946), the Laced Pocket (1946), the Playmaker (1947), the Web Controller (1949), the V-anchored Web (1950), the Trap-Eze (1959), and the Dual Step-Down Palm (1961). Latina's most unusual creation was a six-finger model desiged for Stan Musial so Stan The Man could go from outfield to first base without switching gloves.

When Harry Latina retired from Rawlings in 1961, he was replaced by his son Rollie. It was Rollie Latina who designed the Basket Web and Fastback, which featured a hole through which the fielder could stick his index finger.

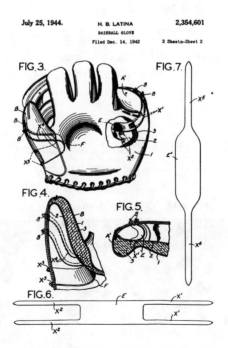

July 25, 1944. H. B. LATINA 2,354,601
BASEBALL GLOVE
Filed Dec. 14, 1942 2 Sheets-Sheet 2

FIG.3. FIG.7.

FIG.4.

FIG.5.

FIG.6.

Figure 5-32A *(U.S. Patent Office)*

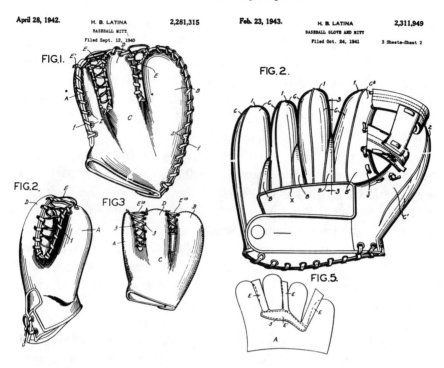

Figure 5-32B   *(U.S. Patent Office)*   **Figure 5-32C**   *(U.S. Patent Office)*

Sixty-two years of Latina glove design came to an end when Rollie retired in 1984. The current Rawlings glove designer, Bob Clevenhagen, is only the third person to hold that position in the company's 109-year history.

▼ *Figure 5-33*   Harry Latina (left) and Rollie Latina (right) show their latest creation to Cardinals third baseman Ken Boyer.

Figure 5-33   *(Rawlings Sporting Goods Co.)*

Stupid Glove Tricks

▲ Buddy Peterson, who played for the White Sox in the mid-1950s, used to tie a rope to his glove and drag it around like a pet dog. After a bad game, he would make the glove sit on the floor in front of his locker all night. Peterson's big league career lasted 13 games.

▲ Before 1954, players would leave their gloves on the field after each inning. Phil Rizzuto supposedly ended that custom one day when he went out to his shortstop position and found a dead rat in his glove.

▲ After a game in the 1970 World Series, a reporter interviewed Brooks Robinson's glove.

▲ Roberto Clemente once threw Bill Mazeroski's ratty old glove into the stands. Fans threw it back.

▲ Whenever he made an error, Minnesota shortstop Zoilo Versalles would throw his glove away. He had to buy new gloves with his own money because the company whose gloves he endorsed refused to give him any more. Nevertheless, Versalles won the Gold Glove Award in 1963 and 1965.

▲ During a game in 1969, Orioles catcher Clay Dalrymple walked out on the field with a catcher's glove on his hand and a fielder's glove in his pocket. He explained to the umpire that if there was a play at the plate, he would like to put on the fielder's glove to make the tag. Request denied.

▲ In 1986, Keith Hernandez of the Mets hit a comebacker to San Francisco pitcher Terry Mulholland. The ball got stuck in the webbing of Mulholland's glove, so the quick-thinking pitcher threw his *glove* to first baseman Bob Brenly. Hernandez was called out. Later, Brenly said, "I should have flipped the glove around the infield."

▲ **Men and Their Gloves.** Former president **George Bush** kept his old Rawlings in his Oval Office desk drawer. One of **Fernando Valenzuela's** gloves is in a Los Angeles time capsule that will be opened in the year 2025. **Babe Ruth** wore a white glove when he was with the Red Sox. **Joe Morgan** was known to use one of the smallest gloves in the game, **Luis Polonia** one of the largest. **Dick Stuart,** a notoriously poor fielder, was known as "Dr. Strangeglove." After his last home game of each season, **Billy Williams** would throw his glove into the crowd at Wrigley Field. Major leaguers generally get four free gloves each season. **Ozzie Smith** would go through a glove every six weeks. The best-selling glove ever was the Rawlings **Dale Murphy** RGB-36.

▲ **Glove Story.** You can't spell glove without l-o-v-e," wrote *Sports Illustrated* in 1990. "The glove is somehow a living thing, like the bud at the end of a stem."

"Players become sexually attached to their gloves," admitted Phil Garner. "A good glove is like a wife," added Dwight Evans. Mrs. Evans has not publicly commented on this topic.

Some players give their gloves affectionate names. Mel Hall calls his "Lucille." George Scott's glove was "Black Beauty" and Aurelio Rodriguez named his "The Black Hand." Ted Simmons named his glove "The Big Trapper."

THE MAKING OF A GLOVE

Baseball gloves used to be made of horsehide, but the switch to cowhide came around 1940. Glove companies use steers because the hide is tough. One baseball glove requires about six square feet of leather.

Since 1960, Rawlings has been turning out 100 to 300 gloves a day at its factory in Ava, Missouri. About one out of three is a catcher's mitt, and one in 12 is for a left-hander. Rawlings makes 75 different models.

▶ *Figure 5-34* The hides are tanned (tan is the natural color) and sliced in half. If an inspector spots any barbed wire marks or tick bites, the hide is rejected.

A glove is made of 15 to 20 pieces of leather. The individual patterns are punched out with a device like a cookie cutter. The strongest part of the hide—the "heart"—is reserved for the pocket (that's why it says

Figure 5-34 *(Collection of Bill Jaspersohn)*

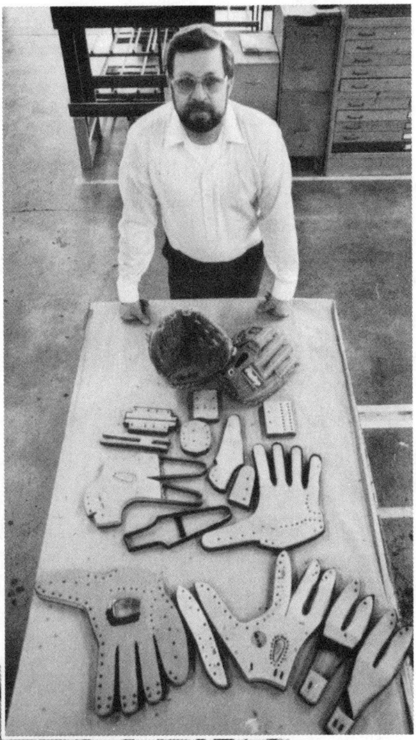

Figure 5-35
(Collection of Bill Jaspersohn)

"Heart of the Hide" inside Rawlings gloves). The belly is used for the lining, the flank for the fingers, and the neck for webbing. While the leather is still flat, it is stamped with the Rawlings logo and glove model.

▲ *Figure 5-35* Next, the leather is pounded by hand with mallets to form a pocket. Strips of dark-blue felt are sewn into the first three fingers. Baseball gloves are sewn together inside out so the stitches won't show.

▼ *Figure 5-36*   The glove is put on a "hot hand," which is a shaped aluminum iron that gets as hot as 300 degrees. It gives form to the fingers and smoothes the leather. After a few minutes, the glove is removed and smeared with sticky wax to keep the leather supple and hold it in place.

The webbing is laced in next. Rawlings has ten different web designs. Many outfielders use a see-through web, so they can hold the glove in front of their eyes as a sun shield while they follow the path of a fly ball.

▼ *Figure 5-37*   Padding is stuffed into the heel of the glove and it's closed up with lacing. Each glove requires 8 to 10 feet of rawhide, and it takes about an hour to sew it all in.

In all, it's a 50-step manufacturing process. Most gloves take nine days to make it through the assembly line, but if Ken Griffey, Jr., for instance loses his favorite glove, Rawlings steps up production. That brings up an interesting conundrum: When your autograph has been burned into thousands of gloves, how can you be sure which glove is *yours?*

In any case, Rawlings glove designer Bob Clevenhagen says, "We could do a single glove in 45 minutes if we absolutely had to."

Figure 5-37   *(Rawlings Sporting Goods Co.)*

Figure 5-36   *(Collection of Bill Jaspersohn)*

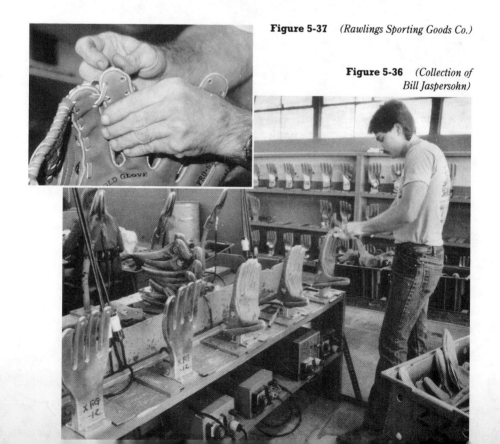

Glove Quotes

"It's a great honor for a steer if his hide is chosen for a glove. It's kind of a posthumous award, however" (Skip Horween, Rawlings treasurer, in *Sports Illustrated*).

"My brother Allie had this left-handed fielder's mitt. He was left-handed. The thing that was descriptive about it, though, was that he had poems written all over the fingers and the pocket and everywhere. In green ink. He wrote them on it so that he'd have something to read when he was in the field" (Holden Caulfield in *Catcher in the Rye*).

"I won't be needing this anymore, Pete" (Lou Gehrig, tossing his mitt to Yankee clubhouse man Pete Sheehy, after his final game).

▼ **What's a Neat?** *Figure 5-38* The time-honored system for breaking in a new baseball glove is to rub it with neat's foot oil. If you think it's cruel to wear dead cow on your hand to catch baseballs, consider that neat's foot oil is the cow's boiled feet and shinbones. The genius who discovered that the stuff softens leather continues to be unrecognized.

In recent years, players have turned to more humane methods to break in their gloves. Robin Yount would throw his in a Jacuzzi. Tony Pena would beat his with a baseball bat. Eddie Brinkman would pour on coffee with cream and sugar. Many players use shaving cream or Vaseline.

Figure 5-38

▼ **The Inflatable Glove.**   *Figures 5-39A, B*   The success of "Air Jordan" and other pumped-up athletic shoes in the 1980s sparked interest in other inflatable sports equipment. State of the art in glove design are models with an internal bladder to provide more protection to the hand and a snugger fit. The patent for Spalding's airFLEX, invented by Alan D. Walker and Andrew Jones, is seen below.

But in fact, the inflatable baseball glove is *not* a recent idea. Catcher/inventor Harry Decker patented the mitt at right in 1906. "In constructing my improved glove I employ an inflatable cushion," wrote Decker, "to provide means whereby it is protected, and, further, to so construct the cushion that it will retain its given shape or contour when inflated."

▶ **Batting Helmets.**   *Figure 5-40*   It's incredible—a game that uses a small, hard object thrown 90-plus mph a foot or two from the player's skull did not make protective helmets with earflaps mandatory until 1974.

While baseball dragged its heels, inventors saw the need for head protection decades earlier and created solutions to the problem. The first batting helmet was invented in 1905 by Frank Pierce Mogridge of Philadelphia. "The use of my invention will not only insure the batter against injury to the head from being struck by the ball," wrote Mogridge, "but will give the batter confidence and prevent him from being intimidated by the pitcher and rendered fearful of being injured by the ball pitched."

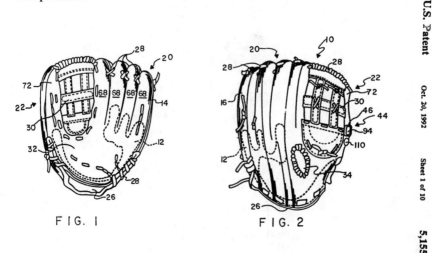

U.S. Patent   Oct. 20, 1992   Sheet 1 of 10   5,155,864

Figure 5-39A   *(U.S. Patent Office)*

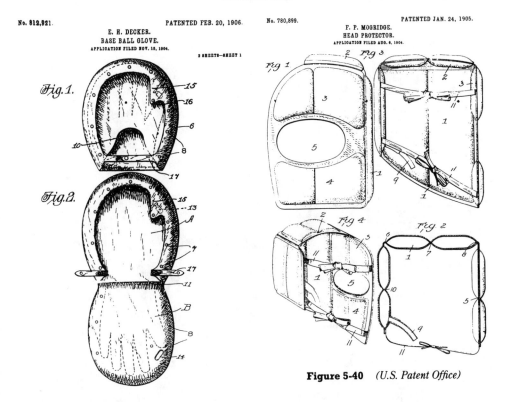

Figure 5-39B *(U.S. Patent Office)*

Figure 5-40 *(U.S. Patent Office)*

▶ *Figure 5-41* Mogridge took his invention to the Philadephia-based A. J. Reach Company, which marketed it under the name Reach Pneumatic Head Protector. Hall of Famer Roger Bresnahan (see "The Father of Shin Guards") used the Head Protector after being knocked unconscious by a pitch from Cincinnati's Andy Coakley, but it never caught on.

As you can see in the ad on the next page, the Head Protector was a goofy-looking device that resembled a boxing glove wrapped around the batter's head. Ballplayers, who until recently had considered it unmanly to use gloves and masks, weren't about to wear something on their head that required a teammate to blow into a rubber tube (9 in the patent drawing) to inflate the thing.

▶ *Figure 5-42* Edward Larkin of Washington, D.C., seems to have modeled his 1932 batting helmet after a turban, or perhaps an upside-down flowerpot. "It is a well known fact that batters become shy of hard pitched balls because of the danger of being struck," wrote Larkin, "and

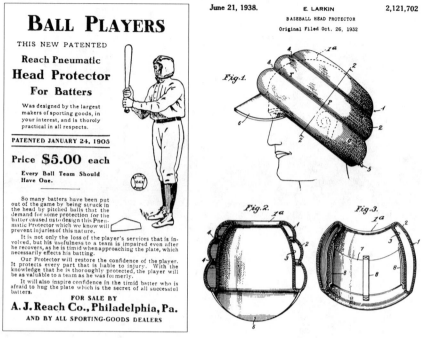

Figure 5-41   **Figure 5-42**   *(U.S. Patent Office)*

it is believed that by providing such a head covering, as proposed in this invention, a great improvement will be seen in their hitting ability." Notice that six years passed between the date Larkin applied for his patent and the date it was granted, presumably to give patent examiners the chance to make copies and pass them around among their friends.

▶ *Figure 5-43*   After Cleveland shortstop Ray Chapman was killed by an underhand fastball from Yankee pitcher Carl Mays (next page) in 1920, there were calls for protective helmets. The Cleveland Indians experimented with modified football helmets in 1921, but the players found them cumbersome. There was an outcry again in 1937 when the career of Detroit catcher Mickey Cochrane was ended by a skull-fracturing fastball from another Yankee pitcher—Bump Hadley. Several players fooled around with polo helmets, and Spalding introduced a device resembling ear muffs, but still, baseball waited.

In June of 1940, 28-year-old Joe "Ducky" Medwick of the Brooklyn Dodgers stepped up to the plate to face Bob Bowman of the Cardinals. Medwick had just joined the Dodgers after seven straight .300 seasons. Three years earlier, he had won the MVP when he led the league in hit-

Figure 5-43 *(National Baseball Library, Cooperstown, NY)*

ting, slugging average, at bats, hits, doubles, home runs, runs, and RBIs.

Medwick and Bowman were former teammates and had argued in an elevator before the game. A pitch got away from Bowman (intentionally or unintentionally) and struck Medwick on the left temple, knocking him unconscious. Medwick recovered, but was never the same again and never led the league in *anything* for the remainder of his career.

Dodger chief Larry MacPhail contacted Dr. George Bennett, a well-known surgeon at Johns Hopkins, and asked him to help create some kind of head protection for hitters. Bennett lacked the expertise, but he called on a colleague at Johns Hopkins, brain surgeon Walter Dandy. With suggestions from Dodger manager Leo Durocher, Dandy designed a set of narrow, curved plastic shields that could be hidden inside an ordinary cloth baseball cap. They were worn by the 1941 Brooklyn Dodgers—the first major league team to wear protective headgear. When Pete Reiser was beaned by pitcher Ike Pearson that season, he suffered no more than a headache. Gradually, however, the plastic shields fell out of favor among the Dodgers.

The Sporting News cites Negro League star Willie Wells as being the first player to wear a batting helmet. In 1942, Wells was hit in the head by a pitch from Bill Byrd and carried off the field unconscious. Afterward he visited a construction site in Newark, New Jesey, and got a worker's hard hat. The next time he faced Byrd, he came to the plate wearing the helmet.

Baseball didn't exactly rush to introduce head protection, but part of the problem was that a successful batting helmet required a material that was very strong but also very light. The first helmets made specifically for baseball were made from *plaster* poured over cloth baseball caps.

Just before World War II, synthetic plastics such as polystyrene and polyethylene were developed. They could be molded into any shape, and they were light, rigid, and tough.

When Branch Rickey left the Dodgers to become general manager of Pittsburgh in 1950, he had a plastic cap made for the Pirates to wear at bat, on the bases, and in the field. New York Yankee shortstop Phil Rizzuto ordered one too. He had been hit in the head once and decided that was enough for him.

Fiberglass was available by the early 1950s, and Cleveland engineers Ed Crick and Ralph Davia used it to design a helmet that weighed just 6.5 ounces. Ralph Kiner of the Pirates was the first to use it in 1952. The following year, Branch Rickey required them for the whole team. Rickey, it is only fair to mention, was the president of American Baseball Cap, Inc., a company that made fiberglass and polyester resin helmets.

By 1955, 14 of the 16 major league teams at least *offered* helmets to their hitters. At the start of the 1958 season, all batters were *required* to wear protective headgear. One of the last holdouts was Ted Williams, who at first refused to wear any protection. "I don't like those space helmets," Williams finally said, "But if I have to wear them, I guess I will."

Helmets with earflaps, which started as a Little League safety precaution, became mandatory in 1974.

▼ *Figure 5-44*   By the time Ted Williams retired in 1960, polycarbonate plastics had been invented. (Now *there's* a sentence you won't find in any other baseball book.) Today's batting helmets are made with a polycarbonate alloy shell, a polyreopylene inside liner, and thermoformed foam earpieces.

The next piece of protective equipment for hitters may very well be a face guard, such as the $15 "Home Safe" in this photo. It was developed by a Salem, Virginia, woman named Lorine S. Caveness whose son was afraid of getting hit in the face by a ball. Charley Hayes of the Colorado Rockies wore a mask like this in 1994 after getting hit by a pitch.

There is some concern in baseball circles that batters now have *too much* protection and have become too bold at the plate. Baseball, they fear, is becoming football.

At the end of his Hall of Fame career, George Kell started wearing a batting helmet. It was Kell who summed it up best when he said, "I may not look so hot in this thing, but I'd rather be alive than pretty."

▶ **Sunglasses.**   *Figures 5-45A, B*   Albert Einstein published the theory of relativity in 1916. The same year Fred Clarke patented a much more significant discovery from baseball's point of view—his invention of flip-up sunglasses.

Fred "Cap" Clarke (next page) got his start in baseball by answering an ad for ballplayers in *The Sporting News*. He went five for five in his first major league game and was a major league manager by the time he

Figure 5-44   *(Face Guards, Inc.)*

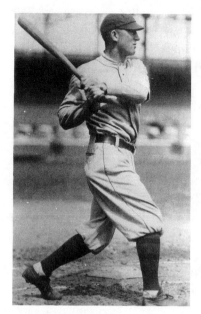

Figure 5-45A *(George Brace)*

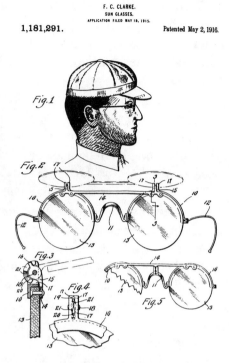

F. C. CLARKE.
SUN GLASSES.
APPLICATION FILED MAY 19, 1915.

1,181,291. Patented May 2, 1916.

Figure 5-45B *(U.S. Patent Office)*

was 24 years old. From 1900 to 1915, he was the hard-driving player/ manager with the Pittsburgh Pirates.

As an outfielder, Clarke hit .312 lifetime and ranks seventh with 220 career triples. As a manager, he guided the Pirates to three consecutive pennants (1901–1903).

Players are seen wearing sunglasses in photos as far back as 1908, but it wasn't until Fred Clarke retired in 1915 that he came up with a simple solution for the problem of putting sunglasses on and taking them off in the heat of the action.

His long-winded description of the invention: "During the playing of a baseball game, certain of the players and particularly the out-fielders are forced to look toward the sun in following a ball batted to the out-field with the result that the fielder is temporarily blinded by the sun, and consequently loses track of the ball, and it is the principal object of my invention to provide glasses having lenses which are connected by spring hinges to the eye-glass frame and which lenses, under normal conditions occupy an out-of-the-way position above the eyes of the player, and are adapted to be instantly swung downward into position in front of the eyes, thereby enabling the player to follow the ball even while looking toward the sun."

This was not Clarke's first invention. In 1911, the year he hit .324 and managed the Pirates to third place, Clarke patented a device that rolled and unrolled canvas coverings to keep baseball diamonds dry. The following year, he patented a sliding pad that was attached to a jockstrap with buttons (see page 230).

▼ *Figure 5-46*   Eight years after he patented flip-ups, Clarke was still haggling with manufacturers to make them, as can be seen from this letter. It wasn't until 1930 that ballplayers were seen wearing flip-up sunglasses. Meanwhile, Clarke made his fortune with oil and ranching in Kansas.

AMERICAN OPTICAL COMPANY

MERRY OPTICAL COMPANY DIVISION

ALSO

MERRY OPTICAL COMPANY

KANSAS CITY, MO.

Mr. Fred C. Clarke,   November 15th, 1923.
% A. J. Spalding Brothers,
Los Angeles, California.

Dear Sir:

Sometime has elapsed since you brought me the sample pair of goggles to be used by ball players, but I have just been able to get the following information:

The factory at Southbridge state that if they are to make these goggles just like your sample it will be necessary to make up special tools which will mean quite an investment. They state it will not be possible to go ahead with this expense on an order for twenty-five pair of goggles and, therefore, the only way they could supply that quantity is to make them up by hand, which would make a very decided difference in the cost.

If you do not feel warranted in placing an order for a greater quantity than twenty-five pair, the factory will make them up by hand at a price of about $5.00 a piece, although this is not quoted as a positive price. This will undoubtedly seem to you like an exorbitant price and, of course, it would be if it were a regular stock article. If you feel you are going to be in position to order any larger quantities and can give us positive assurance about this we will again follow through with the factory and get a price from them taking into consideration the cost of making the necessary tools.

Awaiting your reply, we are

Very respectfully yours,

AMERICAN OPTICAL COMPANY

GFM:EM
Dict. 11-14.

Figure 5-46   *(National Baseball Library, Cooperstown, NY)*

Figure 5-47   *(National Baseball Library, Cooperstown, NY)*

▲ *Figure 5-47*   Fred Clarke wearing his invention. Clarke was inducted into the Baseball Hall of Fame in 1945. He passed away two months before the Pirates won the 1960 World Series.

▲ The first major leaguer to wear eyeglasses on the field was Boston pitcher Will "Whoop-La" White, in 1877. He won 229 games in his career, and 40 or more in three seasons. The first catcher to wear glasses was Clint Courtney, when he was playing for the St. Louis Browns in 1952.

▶ **Ballpark Beepers and Microwave Mitts.**   *Figures 5-48A,B* While chasing a fly ball in 1947, Brooklyn Dodgers outfielder Pete Reiser crashed into the wall at Ebbets Field and was knocked unconscious. It was one of 11 times during his career that Reiser had to be carried off the field on a stretcher. The next season the walls at Ebbets Field were padded and the first warning tracks appeared at Wrigley Field, Shibe Park in Philadelphia, and Braves Field in Boston.

Even with a warning track, outfielders continued crashing into walls and injuring themselves. To solve the problem, Mizuno, the largest producer of baseball equipment in Japan, introduced an "electronic warning track" in 1984. Sensors were embedded in outfield walls. Whenever a sensor detected a human being within a specified distance, the wall would begin beeping insistently.

Figure 5-48A   *(Mizuno)*

Figure 5-48B   *(Mizuno)*

"Some degenerate teams are using infernal machines, rather than honest manual labor with a fungo bat, to propel balls for field practice. And now beeping fences?" wrote an outraged George Will. "If this insensate lust for high-tech baseball does not abate, baseball will become as bad as—this is harsh, but it must be said—football."

For a time in the 1980s, Mizuno was determined to tech up baseball. In 1982 the company introduced the ultimate bad baseball invention—the microwave mitt.

The idea was to make hand signals obsolete. Both the catcher's mitt and the pitcher's glove had a set of buttons on them. If the catcher wanted a fastball, he would press a particular button. This information was transmitted by microwave link to the pitcher's glove. The pitcher would then push a button on *his* glove to accept or shake off the sign.

Furthermore, the manager had a series of buttons in the dugout so he could communicate with his hitter. A microwave transmitter would encode the message and transform it into a synthesized voice that came through a tiny speaker in the hitter's batting helmet.

If you could only bake a *potato* with the thing, it might have been useful. But the microwave mitt was met with such a firestorm of bad press that Mizuno abandoned the idea. If baseball ever adopted electronic mitts, you know dugouts would soon be filled with computer hackers trying to steal signs.

As this book goes to press, outfield walls remain silent and catchers are sticking with the *old* digital system—1 means fastball, 2 means curve.

▼ **The Wireless Outfielder.** *Figure 5-49* Padding outfield fences has served to prevent injuries to daring fielders. Now the problem is outfielders crashing into each *other.* James E. Thompson of Los Angeles came up with this "Baseball Fielders Signaling Apparatus" to solve the problem.

Each of the three outfielders wears a portable radio receiver, complete with an antenna. A coach in the dugout or an "eye in the sky" has a handheld unit that is capable of sending wireless signals to the outfielders' receivers.

U.S. Patent   May 20, 1980   4,203,595

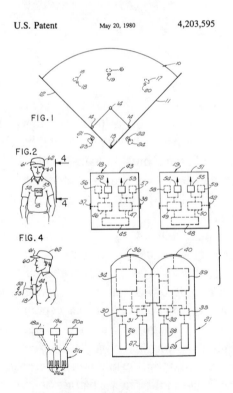

Figure 5-49   *(U.S. Patent Office)*

When there's a fly ball between two outfielders, the coach quickly determines which one has the best chance to make the catch and pushes a button on his unit. The receivers produce "visual, audible, or other sensible signals which can be sensed in some way by the fielder." If all goes well, the player closest to the ball makes the play and the other outfielder backs off safely.

The logical extension of this idea is obvious—robotic outfielders controlled with joysticks. Nobody gets hurt, *no* player has to decide if he can make the catch, and while the initial investment would be costly, the long-term savings in salary would be enormous.

▼ **Uniforms.** *Figure 5-50* A thorough and fascinating history of uniforms can be found in Marc Okkonen's book *Baseball Uniforms of the 20th Century* (Sterling, 1991), but there are a few facts worth mentioning here.

Figure 5-50

For decades, the fabric of choice was wool flannel, which must have been really *fun* to wear on hot summer days. To make matters worse, most teams didn't wash their uniforms every day, especially when they were on the road. Players didn't wear baggy uniforms just because it was the style—they did it for the air-conditioning.

Nylon and other synthetic fabrics were developed in 1938 and started finding their way into baseball uniforms after World War II. Uniforms started getting tighter in the 1960s, when players wore a blend of wool and orlon. Double-knit fabrics, which are even cooler, lighter, more comfortable, and more durable, became popular in the 1970s.

It was probably the popularity of color television in the 1960s that prompted teams such as the Kansas City A's to adopt gold-and-green uniforms. Baseball had the willpower to avoid tie-dyed uniforms, though you can bet the idea must have crossed the mind of Charlie Finley.

▼ *Figures 5-51*   Much of the uniform-making process is still done by hand. Here a worker with Wilson Sporting Goods handles uniform lettering.

Figure 5-51   *(Wilson Sporting Goods)*

▼ *Figure 5-52* The quick and easy way to lose that off-season flab, 1911-style.

▼ **How Do You Play Kangaroo Ball?** *Figure 5-53* Up until the turn of the century, some players were still making their own shoes by hand. But if a young man had seven dollars to spare, he might splurge on genuine kangaroo skin shoes with "porpoise laces."

▶ **Heel Plates and Toe Plates.** *Figure 5-54* These plates, which protected shoes so they would last longer, could be purchased cheaply in the 1880s. Spikes appeared around the same time, to give traction and intimidate opponents. So many players were injured by flying spikes that there was a call to have them banned in 1895. Ty Cobb became fa-

Figure 5-52

Figure 5-53

SPALDING'S SHOE PLATES.

We have experienced more difficulty in the manufacture of a Shoe Plate than any other article that goes to make up a ball player's outfit, but at last we are prepared to offer something that will give the player satisfactory service.
No. 3 0. Spalding's Extra Special Hand Forged Steel Plates, polished and plated, per pair, $0 75
No. 2-0. Spalding's Hand Forged Steel Heel Plates, per pair, 50
No. 0. Spalding's Tempered Steel Shoe Plate, made of imported steel, and warranted not to bend or break; put up with screws. 50
No. 1. Professional Steel Shoe Plate, similar in shape and style to the No. 0 Plate, put up with screws..... .... per pair 25
No. 2. Amateur Steel Shoe Plate, put up with screws....... " 15

PITCHER'S TOE PLATE.

Made of heavy brass, to be worn on the toe of the right shoe. A thorough protection to the shoe, and a valuable assistant in pitching. All professionals use them.

Each............50c.

Any of above plates sent post-paid on receipt of price.

Figure 5-54

SPALDING'S BASE BALL STOCKINGS

Our "Highest Quality" Stockings are superior to anything ever offered for athletic wear, and combine all the essentials of a perfect stocking. They are all wool, have white feet, are heavy ribbed, full fashioned, hug the leg closely but comfortably, and are very durable. The weaving is of an exclusive and unusually handsome design

No. 3–0

No. 3-0. Plain colors. (Colors: feet, white Black, Navy and Maroon. Per pair, **$1.50** order only ; prices on application.) Other colors to

No. 3-0S. Striped, white feet, made to order only, any color. Per pair, **$1.75**

Figure 5-55

mous for sharpening his spikes with a file, but after his career was over he insisted it was a myth.

Today, players use metal cleats for grass fields and plastic cleats for artificial turf. Former Green Bay Packer Mike Tanel, whose football career was ended by a knee injury, has developed a line of cleats with a circular ring on the sole. The circular ring makes pivoting easier, reducing the risk of ankle and knee injuries.

▲ **Why Do Baseball Players Wear Two Socks on Each Foot?** *Figure 5-55* According to legend, Cleveland second baseman Nap Lajoie got spiked badly in 1905 and developed blood poisoning from the dye in his socks. After that, players began wearing white "sanitary hose" under their colored stockings to prevent infection. The name of the person who thought of cutting the colored socks so the white would show through has been lost to history.

▼ **And Finally, the Jockstrap.** *Figure 5-56* There's an old Philadelphia joke that was a lot funnier when the City of Brotherly Love had both the Phillies and the Athletics. It went like this:

One guy: "Are you a Phillie fan?"

Another guy: "No I'm an Athletic supporter."

Placing the male reproductive organs *outside* the body was clearly a cruel practical joke played on the "stronger" sex. A hotfoot from heaven, you might say.

Long before man invented the incandescent bulb, the airplane, the catcher's mask, or any other wonder of the modern age, he perfected the jockstrap. You've got to know where your priorities lie. Players have poked merciless fun at the first ballplayers to wear a mask, mitt, and chest protector. But nobody was ever called a sissy for wanting to protect his private parts. Catcher Claude Berry (1904–1915) has been credited as the first player to use a protective cup.

It is only fitting that this book should end with the jockstrap. There were dozens of patents for "abdominal supporters" in the 1860s and 1870s, but I couldn't resist selecting this one. The inventor was Mary

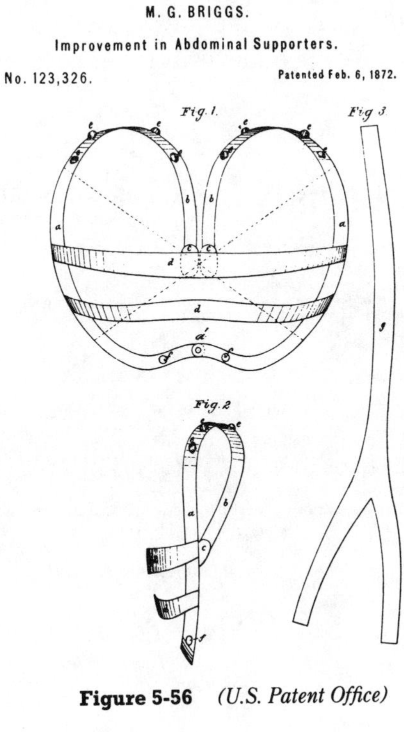

M. G. BRIGGS.

Improvement in Abdominal Supporters.

No. 123,326.   Patented Feb. 6, 1872.

Fig. 1.   *Fig. 3*

Fig. 2

Figure 5-56   *(U.S. Patent Office)*

Georgiana Briggs of Boston, the only female I have come across who was the sole inventor of a baseball product. It is unclear how Briggs's supporter was worn, but she does indicate that it was made of thin bands of steel. Ouch!

▼ **The Anatomically Correct Bike Seat.** *Figure 5-57* The bicycle was a huge fad at the end of the nineteenth century. Apparently, there was some concern that the male anatomy was not compatible with a bicycle seat. In 1895 Spalding acquired the rights to "The Christy Anatomical Saddle," a bike seat with a channel down the middle to protect "those tender parts that are susceptible to injury."

According to popular history the "modern" jockstrap was designed in 1897 by Charles Bennett of the Chicago sporting goods firm Sharp and Smith. They named their product "The Bike Jockey Strap" because it was intended for bicycle riders, who were known as "jockeys" at the time. "Jock" is also British slang for "penis."

The jock has remained pretty much the same for 100 years and has become so popular that its very name is the nickname for athletes, male *and* female. Yet, it's not entirely clear what the thing does. Does the lightweight cloth protect anything? Prevent hernias? Prevent sterility? Or merely get those things out of the way?

Nobody knows for sure. But a few stories of testicles being rammed

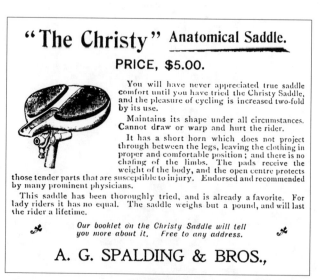

Figure 5-57

into the pelvis are enough to convince most male athletes to wear a jock. During an exhibition game in 1975, Red Sox catcher Carlton Fisk caught a Joe Torre foul tip in the crotch. "Carlton went down as if he'd been shot," said Bill Lee, who threw the ball. Fisk missed two months, then came back to lead the Sox to the pennant. And he was wearing a *protective cup.*

Tom Seaver used to wear *two* jocks, a pair of jockey shorts and a protective cup in the second jock. When asked why *he* wore a jock, tennis star Rod Laver said, "Well, let's just say that when the sun's burning hot you put on a hat."

But not all male athletes wear a jockstrap. Ancient Greek athletes performed their sports in the nude. Sumo wrestlers just wrap strips of cloth over their crotch. Bullfighters, it is said, don't wear a jock because it's macho to expose one's most vulnerable area to the bull's anger.

Only one baseball player—Gashouse Gangster Pepper Martin—was known for playing strapless. "Pepper would play with nothing on under his uniform. No jock strap, no sweat socks, nothing," teammate Enos Slaughter wrote in his autobiography. And Martin was known for his aggressive play and headfirst slides.

▼ *Figure 5-58*   1882. If this is "improved," can you imagine what it improved upon?

▼ *Figure 5-59*   1885. Perfect?

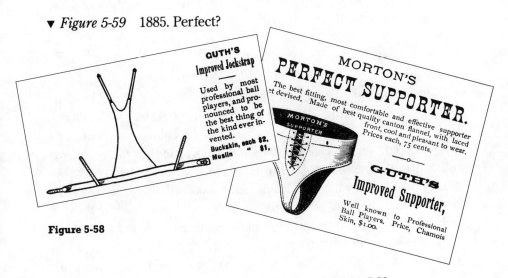

Figure 5-58

Figure 5-59

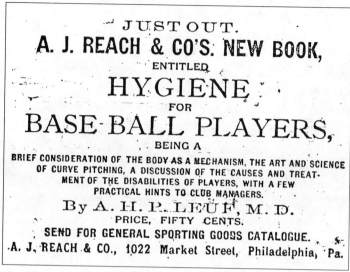

Figure 5-60 *(Sporting Life)*

▲ *Figure 5-60* A must-read for the ballplayers of 1888. Your guess is as good as mine.

▶ **"Unpleasant Sensations"** *Figures 5-61A, B* Sam Morton introduced sliding pads in the 1880s. One of the most famous players of the day, Mike "King" Kelly (seen here), endorsed this and many other products.

▶ *Figures 5-62A,B* Pittsburgh Pirate player/manager Fred Clarke invented a sliding pad that attached to the player's jockstrap with buttons. This 1912 ad states that Honus Wagner was the coinventor, but Clarke took full credit on the patent application. He wrote: "For the protection of the thighs of baseball players in sliding to base it is usual to pad quite heavily the ordinary baseball trousers. This adds to the expense of uniforms because the cost of each pair of trousers is increased by the cost of the padding. Furthermore, the padding detracts from the appearance of the trousers, and again there is sometimes, in the act of sliding, a slipping between the padding and the person of the wearer producing some skin friction and unpleasant sensations."

Figure 5-61B *(National Baseball Library, Cooperstown, NY)*

Figure 5-61A

Today's players wear sliding pads that are built into jockey-style underwear that extends down to the knee. Some even wear sliding *gloves* with padding in them.

▼ *Figure 5-63*   Finally, the perfected jock. This ad appeared in *Baseball Magazine* in 1936.

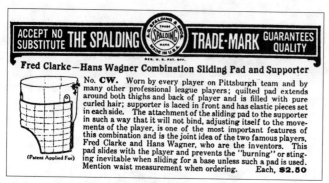

ACCEPT NO SUBSTITUTE **THE SPALDING** TRADE-MARK GUARANTEES QUALITY

Fred Clarke—Hans Wagner Combination Sliding Pad and Supporter

No. **CW.** Worn by every player on Pittsburgh team and by many other professional league players; quilted pad extends around both thighs and back of player and is filled with pure curled hair; supporter is laced in front and has elastic pieces set in each side. The attachment of the sliding pad to the supporter in such a way that it will not bind, adjusting itself to the movements of the player, is one of the most important features of this combination and is the joint idea of the two famous players, Fred Clarke and Hans Wagner, who are the inventors. This pad slides with the player and prevents the "burning" or stinging inevitable when sliding for a base unless such a pad is used. Mention waist measurement when ordering.   Each, **$2.50**

(Patent Applied For)

Figure 5-62A

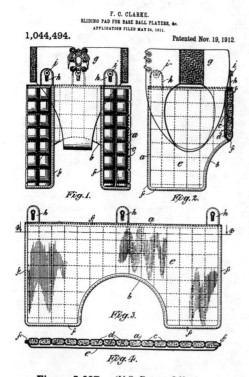

F. C. CLARKE.
SLIDING PAD FOR BASE BALL PLAYERS, &c.
APPLICATION FILED MAY 24, 1911.

1,044,494.   Patented Nov. 19, 1912.

Fig.1.   *Fig.2.*

Fig.3.

Fig.4.

Figure 5-62B   *(U.S. Patent Office)*

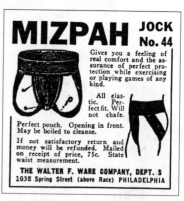

MIZPAH JOCK No. 44

Gives you a feeling of real comfort and the assurance of perfect protection while exercising or playing games of any kind.

All elastic. Perfect fit. Will not chafe.

Perfect pouch. Opening in front. May be boiled to cleanse.

If not satisfactory return and money will be refunded. Mailed on receipt of price, 75c. State waist measurement.

THE WALTER F. WARE COMPANY, DEPT. S
1038 Spring Street (above Race) PHILADELPHIA

Figure 5-63   *(Baseball Magazine)*

Is Any of This Stuff Worth Anything?

"**A**bsolutely," says Josh Evans, the owner of Lelands, a baseball collectibles dealer that has been in business since 1968. "Sports memorabilia is as strong as baseball cards, if not stronger. It's all collectible. Everything sells."

According to Evans, turn-of-the-century bats go for $75 to $200. The price may go up to $1,000 if the bat is autographed. A seat from Crosley Field is worth $2,000; an Ebbets Field seat can fetch $5,000. An old umpire's indicator with five balls and four strikes will sell in the $500 to $700 range. Babe Ruth marketed a line of indicators that were given away with Quaker Oats cereal. Those go for $100 to $200.

"We have a turnstile from Connie Mack Stadium available and it's worth somewhere between $3,000 and $4,000," says Evans. "Catchers' masks from the nineteenth century sell for about $500, even more if they're really unusual or in great condition. Masks from the 1930s to the 1950s sell for $50 to $200. I have old scoreboards worth about $2,500. I just sold a Roberto Clemente batting helmet from the late 1950s for $2,750. I had an indicator used by Bill Klem that went for nearly $1,000."

"Old-time gloves that can be positively dated or belonged to a major leaguer are worth a lot of money," says Alan "Mr. Mint" Rosen, who has been dealing in baseball collectibles for 15 years. "Balls from the

1860–1870 era with different stitching sell for $700 to $2,000, even without autographs. I got $12,000 for an 1898 Brooklyn uniform, and $8,000 for a hat worn by Lou Gehrig."

"It's a very subjective, whimsical value," says Robert Edward Lifson of Robert Edward Auctions. "If something evokes an emotional response because of its history, it's valuable."

So how do you get in on this bonanza as a buyer or seller? Contact one of the following:

▲ Leland's Auction House, 245 Fifth Ave., Suite 902, New York NY 10016 (212-545-0800).

▲ Robert Edward Auctions, P.O. Box 1923, Hoboken NJ 07030 (201-792-9324).

▲ Alan "Mr. Mint" Rosen, 70-I Chestnut Ridge Rd., Montvale NJ 07645 (201-307-0700).

▲ *Diamond Duds: The Newsletter for Collectors of Major League Baseball Uniforms and Equipment.* P.O. Box 10153, Silver Spring MD 20904. A one-year subscription costs $20.

Bibliography

The United States patents reproduced in this book were researched and copied from microfilm at the Government Publication Department of the Free Library of Philadelphia. Most of the old advertisements originally appeared in *Spalding's Official Base Ball Guides* from 1876 to 1905, which have been reprinted by Horton Publishing Company (P.O. Box 29234, St. Louis MO 63126). These are a wonderful chronicle of early baseball, and Horton sells them for as little as $10.

Other valuable information was found in the following periodicals: *Antiques & Collecting, Audubon, Baseball Digest, Baseball Magazine, Beadle's Dime Baseball Guide, Boy's Life, The Cincinnati Enquirer, Cincinnati Magazine, Collegiate Baseball, DeWitt's Base Ball Guide, Esquire, Forbes, Leslie's Weekly, Newsweek, The New York Times, Oldtyme Baseball News, Popular Mechanics, Popular Science, Saturday Evening Post, Smithsonian, Sporting Life, The Sporting News, Sports Illustrated, Time, USA Today, The Wall Street Journal,* and *Yankee.*

And these books:

Adair, Robert K. *The Physics of Baseball* (New York: HarperCollins, 1990).
Alexander, Charles C. *Our Game* (New York: Holt, 1991).
Alvarez, Mark. *The Old Ball Game* (Alexandria, Virginia: Redefinition, Inc., 1990).

Astor, Gerald. *The Baseball Hall of Fame 50th Anniversary Book* (Englewood Cliffs, New Jersey: Prentice-Hall, 1988).

Barber, Red. *1947—When All Hell Broke Loose in Baseball* (New York: Doubleday, 1982).

Bowman, John, and Joel Zoss. *Diamonds in the Rough: The Untold History of Baseball* (New York: Macmillan, 1989).

Davids, L. Robert, editor. *Insider's Baseball* (New York: Scribner's, 1983).

Deutsch, Jordan A., Richard M. Cohen, Roland T. Johnson, and David S. Neft. *The Scrapbook History of Baseball (New York: Bobbs-Merrill, 1975).*

Dickson, Paul. *The Dickson Baseball Dictionary* (New York: Facts On File, 1989).

Durso, Joseph. *Baseball and the American Dream* (St. Louis: The Sporting News, 1986).

Frommer, Harvey. *Primitive Baseball* (New York: Atheneum, 1988).

Goldstein, Warren. *Playing for Keeps: A History of Early Baseball* (Ithaca, New York: Cornell University Press, 1989).

Hughes, Thomas P. *American Genesis: A Century of Invention & Technology* (New York: Viking Penguin, 1989).

James, Bill. *The Bill James Historical Baseball Abstract* (New York: Villard, 1986).

———. *This Time Let's Not Eat the Bones* (New York: Villard, 1989).

Jaspersohn, William. *Bat, Ball, Glove: The Making of Major League Baseball Gear* (Boston: Little Brown, 1989).

Koppett, Leonard. *The New Thinking Fan's Guide to Baseball* (New York: Simon & Schuster, 1991).

Lee, Bill. *The Wrong Stuff* (New York: Viking Penguin, 1984).

Levine, Peter. *A. G. Spalding and the Rise of Baseball* (New York: Oxford University Press, 1985).

Luciano, Ron, and David Fisher. *The Umpire Strikes Back* (New York: Bantam, 1982).

Mazer, Bill. *Bill Mazer's Amazin' Baseball Book* (New York: Zebra Books, 1990).

Nadel, Eric, and Craig R. Wright. *The Man Who Stole First Base* (Dallas: Taylor Publications, 1989).

Obojski, Robert. *Baseball Memorabilia* (New York: Sterling Publishing, 1991).

Okkonen, Marc. *Baseball Memories 1900–1909* (New York: Sterling Publishing, 1992).

———. *Baseball Uniforms of the 20th Century* (New York: Sterling Publishing, 1991).

Okrent, Daniel, and Steve Wulf. *Baseball Anecdotes* (New York: Harper & Row, 1989).

Plimpton, George. *The Curious Case of Sidd Finch* (New York: Macmillan, 1987).

Richmond, Peter. *Baseball: The Perfect Game* (New York: Rizzoli International Publications, 1992).

Salisbury, Luke. *The Cleveland Indian* (Brooklyn: The Smith, 1992).

Schlossberg, Dan. *The Baseball Catalog* (Middle Village, New York: Jonathan David Publishers, 1990).

Seymour, Harold. *Baseball: The Early Years* (New York: Oxford University Press, 1960).

———. *Baseball: The People's Game* (New York: Oxford University Press, 1990).

Shatzkin, Mike, editor. *The Ballplayers* (New York: William Morrow, 1990).

Slaughter, Enos. *Country Hardball* (Greensboro, North Carolina: Tudor Publishers, 1991).

Smith, Curt. *Voices of the Game* (South Bend, Indiana: Diamond Communciations, 1987).

Smith, Ira L., and H. Allen Smith. *Low & Inside* (Garden City, New York: The Country Life Press, 1949).

The Smithsonian Book of Invention (Washington, D.C.: Smithsonian Exposition Books, 1978).

Spalding, Albert G. *Baseball: America's National Game* (San Francisco: Halo Books, 1991, originally published in 1911).

Sutton, Caroline, *How Do They Do That: Wonders of the Modern World Explained* (New York: Quill, 1982).

Thorn, John, and Bob Carroll. *The Whole Baseball Catalog* (New York: Fireside, 1990).

The Timetable of Technology (London: Michael Joseph Limited, 1982).

Voigt, David Quentin. *American Baseball,* 3 vols. (Norman: University of Oklahoma Press; State College: Penn State University Press, 1966–84).

Westcott, Rich, and Frank Bilovsky. *The New Phillies Encyclopedia* (Philadelphia: Temple University Press, 1993).

Wolff, Rick, editor. *The Baseball Encyclopedia* (New York: Macmillan, 1990).

Index

About the Author

Dan Gutman is the author of six baseball books: *It Ain't Cheatin' If You Don't Get Caught* (Penguin, 1990), *Baseball Babylon* (Penguin, 1992), *Baseball's Biggest Bloopers* (Viking Children's Books, 1993), *Baseball's Greatest Games* (Viking Children's Books, 1994) *World Series Classics* (Viking Children's Books, 1994), and *They Came from Center Field* (Scholastic, 1995). He is a member of The Society for American Baseball Research (SABR).

Before turning to the National Pastime, Dan wrote two computer books, founded a video games magazine, and wrote a syndicated column that appeared in *The Philadelphia Inquirer, Miami Herald, Detroit Free Press, Los Angeles Daily News*, and other publications. His writing has also appeared in *Esquire, Newsweek, Discover, Baseball Digest, Science Digest, Writer's Digest, Highlights for Children, Sports Illustrated for Kids, Psychology Today, New Woman, USA Today*, and *The Village Voice*.

Dan has appeared on *The Joan Rivers Show, Entertainment Tonight*, and hundreds of radio talk shows. He also performs as a speaker about baseball for adults and children. In schools, he uses baseball to get kids excited about reading and writing.

Dan Gutman lives in Haddonfield, New Jersey, with his wife, Nina Wallace, an illustrator, and their son, Sam.